Mel Bay Presents

Reaching the Next Level

A Method for the Experienced Classical

Martha Masters

LCCN: 2009925949

1 2 3 4 5 6 7 8 9 0

Visit us on the Web at www.melbay.com — E-mail us at email@melbay.com

CONTENTS

Acknowledgments

Many thanks to the people who contributed in various ways to this book:

Good friends Risa Carlson, Brian Head, Kate Lewis, Michael Partington, Scott Tennant, and Andrew Zohn all responded to my initial inquiry years ago as I was searching for off-the-beaten-path repertoire for my students – this served as the foundation and inspiration for this book.

Dr. Jeff Rinkoff, retina specialist and classical guitar enthusiast, inspired the title of the book over a nice post-concert dinner in Oregon.

My principal teachers throughout my studies gave me insights and inspiration that have lasted throughout the years: Scott Tennant helped me to believe in myself and to discover the power within my playing; Manuel Barrueco taught me how to learn efficiently, and is a model of grace and elegance in music; Jeffrey Meyerriecks introduced me to my first pieces of advanced repertoire, and prepared me to enter college; Michael Mann got me going with my first early performances, competitions and gigs; and Jim McCutcheon, my first teacher, who taught with incredible passion and compassion, and without whom I would never have walked down this path in music.

My GFA colleague and former teacher, Brian Head, provided invaluable guidance throughout this process by supporting and challenging my thoughts and ideas. His incredible and rare ability to see both the smallest detail and the big picture was a great help in making many adjustments to the final draft of this book.

My father, Charles Masters, has been a source of constant support since my early days of studying the guitar. He drove me to lessons, sat with me while I practiced, and provided loving support without pressure. He came to every recital, and supported my decision to pursue a career in classical guitar, which can be difficult for a parent to do. When I finished writing this book, Dad was the first person I asked to read it. Though he is not a guitarist, he is an intelligent and thoughtful person, and someone whose opinion I give the utmost respect. He of course read the book thoroughly, and gave me wonderful, insightful feedback, much of which has been incorporated in the final version of this book. From the bottom of my heart, thanks, Dad.

Just as my father supported me in my youth, my husband, Scott Kugler, has been a source of strength and support for me in my adult life. He was the first to say, "You should write a book"; he is always the first to help me with every aspect of my career, even though frequently it means that it will result in me having to leave town on "business." And when I leave town to play, I know that he is here working hard, and taking care of our children. He is my technical guru, saving me hours of time with his quick computer skills, which are at work throughout the final layout of this book. I couldn't do what I do without him. Again, from the bottom of my heart, thanks, Scott.

Introduction

Why We All Need This Book

This is a book about ideas that are not frequently integrated and discussed in other books, about ideas that can be difficult to put words on. Many topics covered here are those that fall through the cracks when students are learning to play the guitar. Our instrument is a difficult one to learn, and it is easy to miss some of the subtleties of the music; or to recognize them, but to be distracted by the technical difficulties of the instrument. The ideas at the heart of this book are central to playing the classical guitar at a high level, and concepts to which we should all give more thought.

The impetus to write this book was born in my own experiences learning and playing the guitar throughout my career as a student, and now as a professional. The idea developed through my teaching college students and adult hobbyists. Many of us have played for years, but still have old habits (obstacles) that limit our ability to be able to play as we would like. The topics covered here are topics that I not only teach, but that I have lived with every day in my own practice.

Depending on your background (how long you've been playing, and with what level of quality), your obstacles may be large or small, plentiful or few. But the point is, we all have them, every one of us. That's the beauty (and the frustration!) of music – you're never done! There's always something else you can improve, no matter what level you're at. Most of us have at one point or another felt like we've reached a plateau, and no matter how hard you work, there's no improvement. You won't be able to "reach the next level" in your playing until you identify and address your obstacles.

The content of this book is aimed at people who already know how to play the guitar at an intermediate level, all the way up through the most advanced players. This book is for the college student, trying to adjust to the higher expectations often encountered at the university level; for the 40-something lawyer who has played since he was 10, and wants to play a piece as beautifully as he can hear it in his head; for the advanced 16-year-old, who wants to set herself up well for upcoming college auditions, and a career beyond; for the player who has completed formal study, seeking guidance in the process of studying primarily alone.

When you're working on a particular technical skill or interpretive device, it is very important that you choose pieces that are simple enough that you can focus primarily on the technique instead of just trying to "make it" through the piece. So the repertoire in the book, at first glance, may appear "too easy" for you. Perfect. That's exactly what you want. Too many of us spend too much time killing ourselves to learn the coolest, hardest pieces. But if you truly want to improve, that's not going to help you. You need to simplify the elements, to allow you to focus on what you're trying to change in your playing.

Many students have issues with motivation when it comes to working on pieces that are "too easy." I sympathize. So I've tried to select a variety of pieces that are musically satisfying. Since everyone's sensibilities are different, I've also included a list of alternate pieces at the end of the book for further development. I hope this will help with the issue of motivation. The greatest motivation is the improvement you will see if you commit yourself to making changes.

To some extent, the first few sections of this book are chronological. After the discussion about tone, you may wish to skip around a bit. I recommend that you read the beginning of each topic, and listen to your own playing honestly, to see if the subject at hand is an area you need work on. If you feel that your sense of pulse is strong, maybe you'll skip the section on tempo/rhythm and go straight to the section on legato. Be very careful if you skip a topic. Be sure that you really have the right to skip! Be honest with yourself – if you aren't sure, do the work to make sure you understand. Of course, asking the opinion of your teachers/colleagues is a good way to see if you really have earned the right to skip that section.

Through all this, the goal is to help you develop a better ear to critically listen and evaluate your own playing – to become your own best teacher. You may see a teacher one day a week for an hour. A dedicated student puts in six more days of practice each week, often several hours each day. If you aren't skilled enough to "teach" yourself during those hours, your time is being used very inefficiently. Insightful teaching is invaluable, both in your hired teacher, and in yourself.

DEVELOPING CRITICAL LISTENING SKILLS

The first step for you to become your own best teacher is to refine your listening skills. Most method books start with technique, and most students define their level of playing in terms of their technique. But technique is inconsequential if you don't have the ability to analyze what you are doing. The best players are always the best listeners, both when listening to others, and when listening to themselves. For this reason, even before reviewing technique, we will start with developing your skills in listening.

There are many factors that go into having excellent listening skills, including: concentration; having a thorough understanding of the material to which you are listening; listening at a pace that allows you to hear details; keeping an open mind to hear new things; being detail oriented; being able to listen critically to others; and being able to listen critically to yourself.

The best listeners have all of these areas mastered, and probably several others that I haven't listed. Read a bit about each category, and discover where you could use improvement.

DEVELOP YOUR CONCENTRATION

This is probably one of the most important keys to critical listening skills. Without good concentration, you simply will not be able to be a consistent critical listener. One of Webster's definitions for concentration is "direction of attention to a single object." In this case, the desired object of "directed attention" is your playing.

It has become harder and harder for most people to concentrate on anything in our world today. We have a very fast-paced lifestyle, most of us wear many hats: student, teacher, player, daughter, son, parent, significant other, employee, boss, etc. How is it possible for us to settle our minds enough to focus only on one thing when most of us have become such experts at multi-tasking?

> ### Sing the melody as you play.

Good question. And the person who comes up with the easy answer for that will be a rich man. Until someone develops a pill we can take to achieve perfect concentration, here are a few thoughts that may help:

- Always keep a notepad by your practice area. If you have a distracting thought while playing about something you need to do later, stop; write it down; and move on. Trying to suppress these thoughts that pop in our heads is usually futile. Acknowledge the thought, and move on, redirecting your attention to what is at hand.
- Sing the melody as you play (in your head, or out loud). I find that my concentration remains almost flawless when I'm singing, but I may catch myself drifting when I stop singing. Give it a try. Not only does it harness your powers of concentration, but it also dramatically increases your expressiveness. This works not only in the practice room, but on the concert stage as well (though it is generally better not to sing out loud on stage!)
- If your concentration problems are persistent, do some reading on the subject. I have a few favorite books I like to recommend. Much of the content of these books is concerned with performance anxiety as well as concentration, since for many people the topics are related; but the subject of concentration is thoroughly addressed in each book. I have found words in all of these books that really helped me open up and find new ways to think about making music. Sometimes all it takes is a sentence to change your entire perspective; I encourage you to explore all of these books:

The Art of Practicing, by Madeline Bruser

The Inner Game of Music, by Barry Green
The Inner Game of Tennis, by Timothy Gallwey
A Soprano on Her Head, by Eloise Ristad

HAVE A THOROUGH UNDERSTANDING OF THE MATERIAL

I'm no expert on the visual arts, so when I look at a painting, I can't talk much about what makes a painting successful or not in terms of technique – the quality of the brushstrokes; the use of colors. I simply don't have a deep enough understanding, nor do I have the vocabulary to talk about it. If it were my painting, I would have difficulty in knowing how to fix anything in there that wasn't quite working. My problem is that I don't have a thorough understanding of the art of painting.

The same principle applies to music. If you're playing the guitar, obviously you have to have some understanding of the instrument and its repertoire. The more sophisticated a player you want to be, the deeper your knowledge must be in terms of style, technique, and the application of your technique to reach your musical goals.

If you don't understand the basic form of the piece, its basic harmonic structure, its style period and traits of the composer, your musical judgment will be limited and likely awkward. If this is you, it's probably time to hit the books. See the resources at the back of this book for a list a books that may help you learn a bit about styles and how to use that information to guide your interpretation. If you're aiming for a career in music, you will likely have courses in your study that will educate you in this area. If you are an amateur aiming to reach your potential, you may wish to consider taking classes in music history and music theory at your local college. All that you learn in this area will better inform your interpretive decisions, which leads to more effective performances.

> *Practice whatever you can comprehend easily without feeling even slightly confused or overwhelmed. If you aren't truly hearing what's going on, you'll never know how to improve it.*

LISTEN AT A PACE THAT ALLOWS YOU TO HEAR THE DETAILS

This is impossible to control if you're listening to someone else's performance – you can't exactly ask them to slow down or pause so you can better comprehend the details of their performance! But this works well when listening to CDs, or when practicing. When practicing, you can pause or slow down as you are playing to enhance your listening/comprehending abilities; or you can pause the recording when listening back to your own playing as a practice tool (more on that at the end of this section, under Listen Critically to Yourself).

Basically, when things are new, difficult, and/or particularly fast, our brains sometimes just can't keep up. Often the fingers can go, but the brain really doesn't know exactly what's happening. Frequently when I ask a student to slow down a fast passage, she can no longer play it – she doesn't truly understand what is happening, and her fingers are running the show. Not good!

So in your practicing, slow down fast passages. Slow down difficult passages. And with all passages that need better understanding, practice in small segments (a couple measures, a couple beats), whatever you can comprehend easily without feeling even slightly confused or overwhelmed. If you aren't truly hearing what's going on, you'll never know how to improve it.

KEEP AN OPEN MIND

Some people are devastatingly self-critical. They cannot hear the good in their playing, or recognize improvement; their entire focus is on what sounds bad. They may lack self-confidence, or they may think they are doing themselves a favor by being so hard on themselves. To those who lack confidence: you must realize that there is something good to be found in everyone's playing. You must find what that is in your playing, and embrace it. Don't leave this paragraph until you can name a few things about your playing that are good. After every performance, start your self-evaluation with the things that went well. Don't start your evaluation by saying: I missed that scale again; I had a terrible memory slip; etc. Start by listing positive attributes of your performance, such as: I remained calm through difficult challenges; my tone remained consistent; I really communicated the sentiment of the piece; etc. Then, you can begin gently working with yourself on the things that need improvement. Your performances (not to mention your enjoyment of performances) will not improve if you don't have self-confidence and the ability to recognize what you do well.

Some people need to be skeptical of their technique and performance, to ensure that they are playing everything correctly. Always keep a watchful eye on the score, checking for notes or rhythms you may have learned wrong. It's easy to miss an accidental here and there, it happens to all of us. But the more you keep your eyes and ears open throughout the learning process, the more likely you are to catch your mistake. From the technical perspective, if you think you have a great tone, don't take it for granted. Make sure it isn't failing you when you play loud, or fast, or switch to free stroke. If you think you have a great sense of legato, make sure you're still connecting the difficult shifts, as well as the "easy" spots, such as repeated notes on an open string.

Of course all of these thoughts were somewhat pessimistic! Everyone should keep an open mind, looking for the things you need to improve, but also the things you are doing well. It is equally important that you understand your strengths, even if just in one particular piece, so that you know what to continue doing, along with the things you need to change.

An important tangent: Emphasizing your strengths in your performances can help you develop your unique voice, and places your weakness in a more constructive context. This philosophy may help you choose repertoire that is more successful for you. College students and competitors are often somewhat "forced" into playing certain repertoire to pass exams, meet requirements, and prove themselves to be well rounded. Once a player reaches the realm of the professional level, players generally settle into a type of repertoire that best suits their playing, so that they are always putting their best foot forward. Segovia didn't play much avante-gard music; it didn't suit his style. Most of us can readily identify Segovia's sound and his repertoire – he created an identity for himself, perhaps more successfully than any other guitarist to date.

If you're an amateur, you have no requirement to play certain pieces or styles, and you have nothing to prove. Of course you want to continue to improve your playing, and that is what this book is all about. But your repertoire choices can be guided by both technique and your personal sense of style. You can choose pieces that appeal to your sensibilities, that are also well within your technical limits. You can push your technique in exercises and in the practice room, but you should always feel like you have "technique to spare" when you hit the stage.

Now back to listening skills.

BE DETAIL ORIENTED

> *Don't ignore the details- they are at the heart of playing to your potential.*

We'll talk more about specific details later in this book. As we do, those details need to be built into your listening skills. If you accept a certain amount of technical sloppiness, little errors won't ever disappear from your playing. It won't occur to you to stop bass notes from ringing beyond their value if you don't hear how the harmonies interfere with the next chord. It may not occur to you to exaggerate dynamics even more if you haven't given thought to your dynamic plan. So as you develop your understanding of the finer points of playing, you'll have more details to hone in on as you are listening. Don't ignore the details- they are at the heart of playing to your potential.

LISTEN CRITICALLY TO OTHERS

You're a musician. When you go to a concert of any kind, you should listen with a musician's ears. To return to my previous analogy, if I'm at an art exhibit, I look very casually, and simply think, "I like it," or "I don't." If I'm at a concert, of course I have those same subjective feelings. But part of growing as a musician is to understand why you did or did not like it. "I liked their use of dynamics, but he used too much rubato for my taste."…or… "The playing was exquisite, I just thought the programming was a bit slow."...or... "Their tempos were a bit fast, some of the trickier spots were a bit out of control." The more easily you're able to identify these specifics as you listen to others, the more likely you'll be able to identify specifics in your own playing.

LISTEN CRITICALLY TO YOURSELF

If you don't have the above skills, you won't be able to master this skill. You must first be able to concentrate; understand what you're listening for, including details; and be able hear the details in others. Most of us are on a constant quest to improve in all of these areas. The more refined your skills are, the better listener you'll be. There's no limit to your potential, so keep listening!

One of the best ways you can learn to listen critically to yourself is by recording your practice sessions and performances. Get a minidisk, tape recorder, or whatever works for you. It doesn't have to cost a lot of money, but the better quality the recording device, the more details you'll be able to hear in your playing. Start by recording yourself playing one piece. Before you listen back, make sure your score is marked with measure numbers at the beginning of each line. Get a pencil and a piece of paper ready. As you listen, make notes to yourself. To give you an example of what I mean, here is a list I found attached to a piece I studied a couple of years ago. These are notes I took upon listening back to a practice recording:

- m. 13 decrescendo needs to be more exaggerated
- m. 30 scale needs to clean
- Andante section should be slower, more tasto
- Rondo theme needs to be more clear
- m. 45 connect beat 2 to beat 3
- m. 51, more pianissimo, more tasto
- m. 79 don't slow down
- m. 177 slide needs to be clean
- m. 194 harmonic clear

You may need to stop the recording as you're listening to make notes; you should listen a few times. When you're done compiling your list, keep it with your music, and every time you sit down to practice, listen especially for those spots. You may also want to make a light mark in your score (a check mark, a star, whatever symbol works for you) with a pencil to remind yourself of the spots that you need to focus on. You can erase the marks when you've solved the problem. Identifying a problem is the first step to fixing it.

Try this method with any piece you are working on, or one of the pieces in this book as you progress. If you're using one of the pieces in this book, use the checklist as your guide for thing to listen for in the recording. If you are using a piece already in your repertoire, create your own list of things to listen for. This list could include things such as legato connections, bass note damping, technical problems, steady tempo, etc.

THE BASICS OF GOOD TECHNIQUE

> ***Your joints are happiest and healthiest when they are working in their mid-range.***

This book is not intended to be a technical manual, and no book is a substitute for a good teacher. However if we're talking about analyzing your playing, we should at least talk in basic terms about what constitutes good technique. For each of the following categories, I will list some of the fundamental issues to keep in mind where players frequently go wrong. If you've heard any of these concerns from your teacher before, it would probably be a good idea to make sure you make the changes necessary to be playing with good "equipment." You can't run a marathon in high heels; and you can't play the guitar effectively or with longevity without good technical tools.

Your joints are happiest and healthiest when they are working in their mid-range. Avoid over-flexing or over-extending any of your joints; this leads to fatigue, and eventually injury. The best results always come from relaxed, balanced playing. The specifics of how you use your hands (and body) will depend on your physiology, so again, consult with your teacher, and listen to what your body tells you.

Here is a list of things I find myself reminding my students (old and new) of over and over again.

SITTING POSITION:
- Sit up straight.
- Shoulders relaxed. Tension anywhere in your body affects your technical and musical abilities.
- Both feet flat on the ground. I've seen many players who like to prop the right foot up on the ball of the foot (a form of tension); or tuck it under the chair (which causes instability in the positioning of the guitar).
- The neck of the guitar should generally be at about a 45-degree angle. Some people like it slightly higher, which can be advantageous for the left hand. I don't recommend less than a 45-degree angle, because the left hand has a much more difficult job in this position, and most people start to slouch to get their hands in a more comfortable orientation to the guitar.

All pointers for left and especially right hand may vary slightly depending on the size of your hands, fingers, and length of your torso. Again, consult with a good teacher!

RIGHT-HAND TECHNIQUE:
- Your wrist should be relatively straight (not deviating left or right, up or down). This may appear as a slight arch as you look at it from the underside of your arm, as your thumb generally drops creating an arch on the under side. A collapsed wrist doesn't allow you enough follow through and results in a small sound. An over-arched wrist can cause real injury. We want to avoid both!
- You arm rests on the guitar basically in line with the bridge (exactly how far back on your arm depends on length of your forearm).
- All motion for all types of strokes should originate from the large knuckle joint.
- The basic motion is the same for free stroke and for rest stroke. The difference comes in your starting position (where you position your arm to start the stroke).
- For free strokes, your large knuckle joint should be over top of whatever string you are plucking. This will allow you to follow through fully and yet clear the strings behind the string you're plucking. Many people don't quite have the right arm positioned far enough forward to be truly over top of the string with

the knuckle joint when beginning the stroke. This results in a thinner sound and less volume in the free stroke, as well as more tension when trying to play free stroke fast.

- For rest strokes, your large knuckle joint should be 1-3 strings behind whatever string you're plucking (again, depending on length of your fingers. Then your follow through will lead you directly to the next string.
- Having made the previous two points, ultimately, you'll need to be able to play both kinds of strokes from the same position as a matter of practicality (there's often simply not enough time to move back and forth quickly within a phrase). Though this contradicts everything I just said, there's no way around it! Generally, it's easier to air on the side of your free stroke position, and learn to play rest stroke from there. Work with your teacher on that.
- Be sure you can distinguish the difference in arm position when switching between rest stroke and free stroke positions.
- Pluck off the left tip of the finger/nail. Aim for simultaneous contact with flesh and nail – it softens the attack, and yet allows for great clarity. Be very consistent about your attack point. These are critical factors to having a great sound.
- When working on your free stroke, it is best to exaggerate the follow through in your initial practice, to make sure you really get the full range of motion in the finger. The steps of a free stroke should be:
  - o Plant (find your perfect contact point)
  - o Pluck
  - o Follow through all the way to your palm. This motion is an exaggeration – but useful to make sure the upper portion of the finger is also involved in the follow through motion. Once you're sure you are moving from the large knuckle joint, you can relax into a more normal follow through.
  - o Immediately empty the tension from your finger. It should naturally rebound just in front of the string you just plucked. All other fingers should be relaxed during the stroke; there may be some sympathetic motion. You may wish to plant your thumb to use as an anchor while doing this.
- The steps for a rest stroke are the same, but instead of the follow through all the way to the palm, the follow through ends on the adjacent string.
- The steps of plucking and following through were probably fairly "combined" from the beginning – inertia causes that. Next step is to make sure that your release of tension after your follow through is immediate. (It should really be done this way from the beginning; but many players tend to hold the finger in the follow through position before releasing.) The pluck, follow-through and release should essentially be reflexive motions. Finally, once you can do these steps consistently and with confidence, you'll want to start to reduce the amount of time spent planting on the string before the plucking motion begins. Make sure that you are confident in your attack point before you begin this process. But you'll never be able to play truly legato until you can make the step of the plant instantaneous with the pluck.
- To Plant or Not to Plant: Now you know what planting is (finding your perfect contact point on the string). You may hear people talking about planting as a technical tool. My take on this is that absolutely, we should all plant (or "prepare") our strokes, every single one. And as a part of slow practice, often that will mean the right-hand fingers rest on the string before plucking, momentarily stopping the vibration. However, as part of playing truly legato, the planting part of the stroke must become so quick that it is inaudible. This leads to what I sometimes call "unprepared strokes." A more accurate term for it (though quite a mouthful) would be "instantaneously prepared strokes," as it is impossible (and undesirable) for the finger not to touch the string at all before plucking. The planting motion simply becomes instantaneous, but if your technical foundation is laid well, the contact point is still solid. So, to plant? Yes. Just do it very quickly!
- The best way to work on the right hand is to play open strings very slowly (perhaps quarter note equals 50, playing every other click). Watch your right hand closely as you play; be very sensitive to how things feel as you play them; be very sensitive to the sound you are producing. If something doesn't work, the slow tempo allows you time to analyze what you didn't like, and try another approach on the next stroke. Gradually refine until you are consistent with your strokes. Always aim for great tone, great projection and great consistency.

LEFT-HAND TECHNIQUE:

- Many people find it easiest to define their left-hand position with the hand in seventh position, as the arm tends to hang most naturally there. I'd recommend starting by checking your left hand in this position, by placing your fingers (1-4) on the first string, frets 7-10.
- The wrist should be straight, not deviating left or right, up or down.
- The inside of your palm should be parallel to the neck of the guitar; relatively close to it, but not quite touching; and on approximately the same plane as the neck (not too much above or below the neck). This last direction may change a bit as you play lower strings – you may need to come slightly above the plane of the neck of the guitar.
- Your arm/elbow should be wherever it needs to be in relation to your body to support the wrist/palm position. Common mistakes: holding your elbow in tight to your body (deviates the wrist); pushing your elbow out too far from your body (doesn't allow the inside of your palm to remain parallel to the neck).
- Your thumb (generally resting on its tip joint) should be midway between the first and sixth strings on the back of the neck. The thumb should always be one fret higher than whatever position you're in. For example, if you're playing in seventh position, the thumb should be behind approximately the eighth fret. Playing with the thumb too far to the left results in less balance and strength for the third and fourth fingers, which are already at a disadvantage for most of us.
- Fingers should remain completely independent of one another at all times. For example, avoid the second finger "attaching" to the first finger when the first finger plays.
- All fingers should remain slightly curved (watch especially for the fourth finger), as locking the joint results in loss of control. Keep a close eye on your tips joints, and the middle joints on your third and fourth fingers, as those are most likely to collapse if your left hand isn't well trained.
- Generally speaking, we want to play on the tips of the fingers. Playing too far on the pads of the fingers results in interference with adjacent strings, which is a problem when we're playing multiple voices. My second and third fingers develop calluses in the center of the tips; my first finger has a callus also on the left of the tip, and the pinky also has a callus on the right side of the tip (as I look at my hand in playing position). This results from how the fingers make the shape of a fan as they all approach the frets together. Exact placement of the finger will depend very much on the situation.
- A common problem with the left hand is excessive tension. The key to solving this is awareness. More on the concept of awareness in the section on Gaining Control of Your Technique. For now, do a little exercise where you start with one finger (any finger, fretting any note) using almost no pressure in the left hand, while plucking the string. Gradually increase pressure with the left finger until you reach a clean sounding note. You may be surprised at how little pressure it takes to sound a note cleanly. If excess tension is a problem for you, work on your awareness of it. The change can only come with dedication and slow practice.
- Another common left hand issue is excessive movement of fingers when not in use. Fingers should remain close to the fretboard at all times, not "releasing" one to two inches away from the neck. This is generally a sign of tension, and takes you far out of "ready" position. The best and fastest players often look like their fingers are hardly moving. Practice releasing tension from a note, and allowing the finger to hover over the fret it just played while moving on to the next note.
- Shifting is also a big problem for many, even those with a well-developed left hand. As you shift, the way in which you use your hand must remain the same. Otherwise, you're practicing with too many different techniques, reducing your experience with any one method, thus reducing your accuracy. As you shift, make sure the arm moves to support the position your hand requires. Make sure the thumb moves with you (and not behind the speed of the shift).
- Another problem often encountered while shifting is that many players tend to feel rushed, and grab at the new chord, which never feels or sounds very good. The best solution to this is to break down the move into a five-part process. 1. **Play** the first chord; 2. **Release** the tension (don't move yet); 3. **Shift** to the new position (but don't grab the chord); 4. **Reapply** tension on the new chord (but don't pluck yet); 5. **Play** the new chord. Do this several times methodically with a metronome. When you feel completely relaxed with the shift, gradually start combining the steps (Play/Release; Shift; Reapply; Play….then Play/Release; Shift/Reapply; Play….then Play/Release/Shift/Reapply; Play….then the entire shift in one

move). If you are methodical about this, and perfect each process before moving on, your shifts should relax and improve dramatically.

- The best way to practice basic left-hand position is by doing simple chromatic scales (you shouldn't be worrying about what note to play next – keep it as simple as possible so you can focus on the technique). Start in one position on one string. When you're reliable with that, then try it across three strings; then across six strings (notice how your hand may change slightly in relation to the plane of the neck of the guitar when you cross six strings). Then try shifting while playing on one string; then try shifting on a scale across three strings; then across six. Each of these adds a level of complexity which you'll need in order to be able to play advanced repertoire, but which you must first master at the fundamental level.

- After making all these points, remember, there are examples where virtually all of these "rules" can (and should) be broken. Think of these rules more as guidelines, and if you feel the need to break them, be clear about why, and check with your teacher.

One final important factor to consider is that the more consistent you are with how you use your hands, the more accurate you'll be. If your hands are constantly approaching the guitar from a different angle, your job is infinitely more difficult. Your technique sets the ceiling for your performing abilities. If you have limits to what you can do, you must address these fundamental elements in order to gain control, accuracy, and speed.

> *The more consistent you are with how you use your hands, the more accurate you'll be.*

Learning New Repertoire
with Good Study Habits

If you don't have good listening skills, it is difficult to have good study habits. A big part of efficient study habits is knowing when you need to stop and fix things, so be sure that you've considered the issues in the section on Critical listening before reading on.

Once you are able to listen to yourself critically, we can start the process of improving study habits. Our discussion here will focus on learning a new piece. The number one mistake many players make is spending too much time running through the piece, playing it beginning to end. This should be a very small percentage of your practice time, particularly when first starting a piece.

Gain a General Understanding of the Piece

When you get a new piece of music, of course you need to read through it to get an idea for what the piece is about musically, discover the technical challenges, and understand what you are getting in to. After the initial readings, the next step is to establish basic fingerings that support your musical plan for the piece (more discussion to come on fingering choices in a later section). I generally try to finger the entire piece on a basic level before working too hard on any one section, as sometimes I'll discover a passage later in the work that may change my mind about an earlier fingering. This work can be rewarding if you have good fretboard knowledge, or painful if you don't (or if the piece is particularly difficult to read). Of course, the fingering process will continue as you get to know the piece better, and you are bound to make changes as you go. But I believe that you must have an overall plan before digging in on any one area too deeply. During this process, you'll also get to know the piece a bit more, and understand where you think there might be climaxes, section breaks, etc. All of this will come into play as we move forward.

Divide and Conquer

After your general plan for the piece has taken shape, you'll be ready to start in with detailed technical work, for your fingers to learn how to make their moves with efficiency, and, eventually, in tempo. I always write in major phrase marks, which not only help me understand the piece musically, but also guide me in terms of breaking the piece down into manageable sections for practice.

Once you have divided your piece into sections, it is very tempting to start in the beginning of the piece. However, I would recommend that you start with the most difficult section. If that happens to be the beginning, fine. But if there is a section with a lot of shifting, barring, fast scales, or difficult counterpoint, it would be wiser to start there, and have more time in the span of your work on the piece to "live" with that section.

I generally devote a couple of days to each section, making sure my fingers can move at a steady tempo, with only planned hesitations, before moving on and working on the next section. I don't try to completely master every section up to tempo before moving on; but rather to make sure the quality of my technique is solid, and that I'm clear about what I'm doing. Once I get it, I move on to the next section. I learn the entire piece this way, and by the time I've done all the sections in this manner, I have a better idea for how the piece is working for me (where are my difficult spots; which sections are still well below tempo, which are coming up to tempo more easily).

Getting It Performance Ready

The next phases of learning a piece generally take the longest, in my opinion. We must bring things up to tempo; clarify the musical plan; and in some cases, we want to memorize it as well.

Memorization is a large subject of its own, which I highly recommend you check out the writings of Aaron Shearer, in his book called *Learning the Classic Guitar, Part 2* (MB#94362), published by Mel Bay. He covers the topic so thoroughly that I would have little to add. My only bit of wisdom on the subject that I want to highlight here is that you should be sure to memorize your music from multiple perspectives. Some people memorize most naturally in a physical manner, their fingers remember with repetition; some people memorize more by the sound; some people have a clear visual picture of the score; others memorize each voice individually and how it moves. We all tend to gravitate to one method naturally; all methods have advantages and disadvantages. The more you develop the other styles of memorization, the more backup you'll have in case your primary mode of memorization fails you in the heat of the moment. Don't rely strictly on physical memory; or strictly on an intellectual understanding. The more different ways you approach the memorization, the more thorough your true understanding of the piece, the more solid your memory.

Bringing a piece accurately up to tempo requires great technical devotion, and use of your Critical listening skills. I have found the heavy use of a metronome very helpful. In playing the guitar, it is critical that you make quality and purposeful motions with both hands, and avoid confusion. Assuming you're doing that, sometimes you may have "hesitations" you've built in during the learning process to accommodate that goal. Obviously, you have to work those out if you're going to perform the piece! So, how to do it...

SPOT PRACTICING

I can't overemphasize the importance of this practice technique. If you have a difficult shift, practice just those two chords, until you can do it in a relaxed, accurate manner at a slow steady tempo. Then back out and make sure you can do the entire measure at a slow steady tempo. Then put the metronome on, and gradually work up that slow steady tempo to fit in with the tempo of the surrounding section. Same goes for any difficult spot. Start by allowing yourself the hesitation as necessary to make a quality move; gradually work out the hesitation, keeping the quality motion at a slow tempo; then speed it up. Whatever you do, don't play it faster than you can do it accurately.

The first time I took this spot practicing method to an extreme was in preparing a very difficult piece by Rodrigo for a competition. It was full of long, fast scales, which were most definitely my weakness; and I only had a couple of months to learn the piece. I was amazed at how the scales in this piece came together for me, with a lot of focused practice. I kept a tally sheet, and did each scale (at whatever my quality tempo was at that point) ten times in the morning, and ten times in the afternoon. I developed a wonderful quality muscle memory, my fingers virtually never made a wrong move. Though I started out slow, the tempo came up, and in short time I had the most accurate (and fast) scales of my life.

...make quality and purposeful motions with both hands, and avoid confusion.

I was hooked on this method of practice, which surely my teachers had been trying to get me to do all my life. I think what helped me to finally commit to doing this (besides the pressure of competing at the international level) was my teacher at the time, Scott Tennant, suggesting I literally keep a tally sheet. It helped me to be accountable for repetitions, instead of saying "I did it well twice, it must be good." I found the tally sheet to be remarkably helpful, and I still use it in my practice today. I suppose you could liken it to a dieter counting calories; or a weightlifter counting repetitions. We need to be accountable for doing it right more than just once or twice if we want to be able to rely on playing it accurately under pressure. Most important if you use this method: make sure the repetitions are quality – otherwise, you're simply drilling mistakes, which guarantees disaster.

KEEP THE QUALITY OF LEARNING AT A HIGH LEVEL

Back to generalities about learning a new piece. You could speed up the process of learning a piece by doing only one day per section instead of two or three days; or doing two sections per day. But I've found that I generally prefer to spend more time reviewing other sections, or working on other repertoire, than "cramming" to learn a new piece. This is a personal preference. If you love to devour new music, then maybe you would enjoy the cramming! Just be sure if you do this to keep the quality level high.

I've found this sectionalized method of learning to be particularly helpful when I have a long or challenging piece

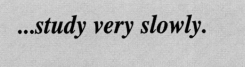

...study very slowly.

that I find intimidating. Sometimes, the appearance of the music on the page can be so overwhelming, it can be a daunting task just to begin. Breaking up the task into manageable sections helps greatly with the intimidation factor.

Through every step of this process, it is critical that you play with complete control and purpose. If you grab at chords as you're trying to finger the piece, you're establishing poor quality muscle memory; and your fingers have a powerful memory of what they have done, for better or worse. So make sure that at all times, you are moving with purpose. This generally requires that you study very slowly. Something you've likely heard many times from your teachers; and you'll hear many times throughout this book.

GAINING CONTROL OF YOUR TECHNIQUE

It can be difficult to strike a balance between developing your musical skills and your technical skills. Most of us seem to have a gift for, and enjoy practicing more, one area or the other. If you enjoy working on technique, good for you. Keep reading to make sure you're doing it in a high quality manner before deciding to skip this section. If you don't enjoy it, and don't often practice technique, you know this section is for you.

RELAX!

Before you can obtain a truly solid technique, you must be completely relaxed, in every part of your body. This doesn't just mean your hands, and your shoulders, which most players are already aware of. But also your feet (do you prop up on the ball of your foot sometimes?), your toes (do you curl your toes?), and especially, your face. Tension anywhere in the body takes away from where we need to be focusing our mental and physical energy. Don't underestimate the importance of a truly relaxed body in your playing.

> *Before you can obtain a truly solid technique, you must be completely relaxed, in every part of your body.*

If you have issues with tension, I highly recommend that you get to know your body better. The more in touch you are with points of tension and how to relax them away from the guitar, the easier it will be to detect tension when it creeps in to your playing, and to release it. One of the best ways to improve your awareness of tension is through exercise. Many musicians find courses such as yoga and Tai Chi very useful; Alexander Technique has also taken off as a popular way to raise awareness in this area. But even if you're not interested in pursuing one of these methods, simple exercise, such as walking, jogging, or stretching, helps you gain awareness of your muscles, and their states of tension and relaxation. Awareness is the first step towards solving the problem. If you don't sense the tension, you have no chance at releasing it. If you don't have good control of your muscles, you also have no chance at releasing tension in them while playing.

One of the most persistent forms of tension that I see (and that I suffered) is in the jaw. If this is something that affects you, start practicing with your mouth slightly open. Not wide enough to catch flies, just slightly ajar. It will prevent the jaw from clenching, prevent the lips from pursing, and help you to breathe a bit more naturally through the mouth as you begin to work on breathing (more about that in a later section).

HAVE A CLEAR GOAL IN YOUR TECHNICAL EXERCISES

When doing technical exercises, it is important that you don't go on autopilot and do the exercises just so you can check them off your list. If you're practicing scales every day, what is your purpose? Your primary goals with every note you play must be great tone (more about that later) and accuracy. So if you're playing the scales with great tone and accuracy, why should you keep practicing them? Are you playing

> *Determine your goal; then use your critical listening skills to make sure you're working towards it.*

truly legato? Are the shifts done in a relaxed and efficient manner? Are you working on speed development? Make sure there is always a goal to your technical practice. Don't just do it so you can brag to your friends that you practice one hour every day on scales. Technique practice is a waste of time unless you have a goal. Determine your goal; then use your critical listening skills to make sure you're working towards it.

Everyone must find their own routine, and what works for them. If you hate practicing scales for the sake of scales, choose a piece with some scales in it, and suddenly you have a reason to practice them. Don't worry if you don't have then entire set of Segovia scales under your fingertips. It's the skills you acquire by studying the technique that matters. The same goes for arpeggios, tremolo, etc. You can practice technique through your repertoire, as long as you do it intelligently.

Do What Works for You

In the Resources section, you'll find a list of a few technique books that you may find interesting. If you like the idea of having a technical routine outside of your repertoire, you may wish to take a look at one or more of these books, and see which one(s) captures your enthusiasm. Without a passion for practicing it, you won't maintain a commitment to regular technical practice.

You don't have to do every exercise in a book. Determine what your weaknesses are, and seek out exercises to develop those areas. You may use a few exercises from three different books; you may create your own exercises; you may exclusively excerpt from your repertoire to build your exercises. Your Critical listening skills have probably revealed some areas you need to work on. Don't ignore them, or try to treat them with sheer will. Address them systematically, and you have a better chance at eradicating the bad habits from your playing.

In the end, when you apply what you've learned in your technical practice to your repertoire, the most important things you can remember are:
- Slow down
- Listen

Don't leave your good technique in the technique portion of your practice session; make sure you study your pieces slowly and carefully enough to apply your good habits. If you're one who constantly wants to tackle the most difficult pieces, take time out to step back now and then and make sure that your technique can handle the repertoire you are playing. Look for repertoire that is interesting, but allows you to manage your technique and have enough control left to be expressive at the same time.

> *Look for repertoire that is interesting, but allows you to manage your technique and have enough control left to be expressive at the same time.*

You shouldn't be working on the Aranjuez unless you can *master* a piece such as this Prelude by Reginald Smith Brindle (and many others as well!). And I do mean master – use good study habits to get this piece under your fingers; and use your developing Critical listening skills to pick apart your performance of this piece.

STUDY TIPS

- In measure 1, be sure to make clear decisions on your right-hand fingerings, and where you'll use slurs (if you choose to slur). Otherwise, this run will be very difficult, or at best, inconsistent in your performance.
- Don't play the piece faster than you can play the runs cleanly, and in control.
- Practice with a metronome to make sure you're getting the rhythmic relationships right.

ETRUSCAN PRELUDE NO. 1

Reginald Smith Brindle
b. 1917

Tempo libero (con fuoco e passione)

Every student wants to play Recuerdos de la Alhambra as soon as they hear it, and why not, it's a great piece. But tremolo is a difficult technique to master, and Recuerdos has many complications inherent to the piece itself. If tremolo is a new technique for you, or one which you need more work on, don't tackle one of the most difficult tremolo pieces in the repertoire on your first attempt. Start with a work that is shorter (endurance is a factor in tremolo), and more manageable. This beautiful work by Viñas is a great place to start. The degree of difficulty for the left hand is much simpler than in Recuerdos, allowing you to focus your attention on your tremolo, and how well it's working for you.

STUDY TIPS

- Measures 1 and 5: Don't let the open G bleed over into beat 3 (use rest stroke to block the string).
- Measure 3: Be careful with the rhythm.
- Measure 7: Be sure to connect these chords – strive for true legato.
- Before beginning to play the tremolo within the piece, work on the entire tremolo section for left hand security by playing the chords without the tremolo. For example, measures 9-10 would be played:

- Practice with dynamics in the early stages, even before introducing the tremolo. This will ensure that the phrasing develops naturally alongside the technique.

- When tremolo is on second string, be sure you are not striking the first string intermittently. If you have this problem, isolate your tremolo technique and practice it exclusively on inner strings until you've resolved the problem before playing tremolo within the context of the piece.

- Use your Critical listening skills to detect any undesired sounds in the tremolo, such as a naily tone, uneven rhythm, or certain notes sounding louder than others unintentionally.

SUEÑO

(Reverie)

José Viñas
1823-1888

22

23

Playing with a Consistent, Beautiful Tone

Consistent and beautiful tone production is arguably the most important key to great playing. If you can play outrageously fast and accurately, but have no control over the tone quality of each note, it will never be very nice for the audience (even if *you* have learned to live with your sound). In an ideal world, I would have put this section first. However, if you haven't developed your Critical listening skills, you may not be able to discern how good or bad your tone is. If you haven't developed a bit of patience, you'll have no chance at slowing down enough to address any possible changes in tone. And if your right hand isn't working well, you most likely won't have a good or reliable tone.

Knowing that you need to work on your tone is a great starting point, but it's not enough to know that it's bad. You need to know what to do specifically to make it better. Three key issues involved in making a good, consistent tone are: nail care, hand position and follow-through. We'll talk about each one individually, and hopefully you'll be able to identify which area(s) you need to work on to get the sound you dream of.

> *You must buff your nails every time you sit down with the guitar.*

Great Nails

If your nails are in bad shape, you can be doing everything else right, and it still won't sound good! One of the most common problems I see is that many players don't buff their nails every time before playing. Buffing yesterday won't cut it; or even in the morning, if you're practicing in the afternoon. You must buff your nails every time you sit down with the guitar. And sometimes even between pieces if your strings are old (the trebles can get scratched and put small nicks in your nails), or you are playing a lot on the bass strings. Don't file every day – you'd lose too much length. But use the smoothest part of your buffer, or very fine sandpaper, just to make sure that there is nothing that can catch on the string. When you buff, make sure to cover the entire playing surface: on the top side, the under side, and straight on the edge. The "edge" of the nail should be as round as possible for a round sound.

Keep a buffer in your guitar case, by your music stand, and in your briefcase, backpack, and/or purse; so that you can always keep your nails in great shape. Letting little nicks in the nail accumulate increases the likelihood of catching the nail and ripping it.

If you're a good buffer, then the issue may be nail shape. Most players who are at a point of reading this book already have an idea of how to shape your nails. If you're having an issue with tone on a certain nail, you may try experimenting with the length just a bit. If you're a bit too naily in your sound, try shortening the length. If you don't have enough clarity, try your nails a bit longer. Don't be afraid to experiment – nails grow back. Just try not to do it the week before a performance!

Some people are blessed with great nails for the guitar, and never have to worry too much about the subject. Others have issues, the worst of which I've seen is hooking nails (nails that curve downward). These seem to be the toughest to deal with in guitar playing. With any sort of nail problems, you should work closely with your teacher; talk a lot with other guitarists; read a lot of articles on the subject. But in the end, you must find the solution that works best for you. Most players with really difficult nails end up using a permanent solution of some sort of fake nails (ping pong balls; silk; acrylic; or the latest I've seen, custom finger nails that apply with glue dots – expensive, but highly effective).

Whatever it takes, make sure that you can produce a beautiful quality sound with each of your fingers individually before addressing tone production while playing a piece of music.

CONSISTENT HAND POSITION

The second issue I mentioned as being critical to good tone production is hand position. Generally, most pedagogues agree today that the best position for your hand is to approach the strings with a straight wrist, not deviating left or right. Due to where we generally plant the arm on the guitar (near vertical alignment with the bridge), that leads most players to a somewhat natural approach to playing off the left side of the fingernail. This position produces a warm, full sound (when combined with good nails and good follow through), which works well as a basic tone. Of course, periodically it is musically desirable to mix up your sound just a bit. But don't experiment with other sounds until you have your basic tone, the one you'll play one the majority of the time, mastered. If your wrist doesn't hold a steady position, spend lots of time on simple exercises that can be memorized, allowing you to watch your right hand, and learn to keep it steady. Refer back to the section on The Basics of Good Technique for further guidance.

FOLLOW THROUGH

Finally, follow through. If you have great nails, a good and steady hand position, you are probably getting a reasonable sound. But if you aren't following through convincingly, it will always be a small, weak sound. The number one fear behind most players who don't follow through is accidentally striking the next string when playing free stroke. Sometimes, this is a baseless fear. You have to try it to know whether or not you'll hit the next string. So, try a few free strokes, exaggerating the follow-through all the way to your palm (followed by immediately releasing tension in the finger). Try it slowly, to really feel how the finger moves. If you don't accidentally strike the next string, then you're OK. You just need to work on your comfort level with doing it.

If you do strike the next lower string, then you'll need to make a slight adjustment in your hand position. Generally, your large knuckle joints should be directly above whatever string you're plucking when playing free stroke (for rest stroke, large knuckle joints are a couple of strings behind whatever string you're plucking). To achieve this, you can generally just slide your arm slightly forward on the guitar. Again, refer back to the section on The Basics of Good Technique for further guidance.

Once you've got these three issues under control, you should be capable of producing quality, consistent tone. If you had to make changes in any of these areas, or especially in more than one area, don't expect to be able to apply your new tone in your pieces overnight. It will require a lot of work on open strings, then in simple exercises, and with your pieces played very slowly, to be able to realize the changes in your playing at tempo.

Whatever you do, don't give up. A solid player with a poor tone will never be a great player. Demand the best, using your Critical listening skills.

> *A solid player with a poor tone will never be a great player.*

- There are several options for how to finger the right hand (the fingering suggested is based on maintaining the most replicable pattern that will last throughout the piece), but whatever you decide, be sure to be clear about what you are doing, and be consistent. This piece is deceptively easy, but if you are remotely inconsistent about your right-hand fingerings, you will develop poor muscle memory and will never be able to consistently perform this piece. I strongly recommend that you write in right-hand fingerings for every note of this piece. This is an extreme but effective means of establishing consistency.
- Be sure to keep your slurs rhythmically even and strong.
- Connect all quarter notes in all voices (sustain them above any eighth notes that occur in other voices).
- Be careful of a few left hand issues in measures 13 and 18-22. Using your left hand very wisely will help make these passages easier.
- Listen for your beautiful tone in the melody!

á Norbert Dams

ALLEGRO MODERATO

from *Five Vignettes*

Atanas Ourkouzounov
b. 1970

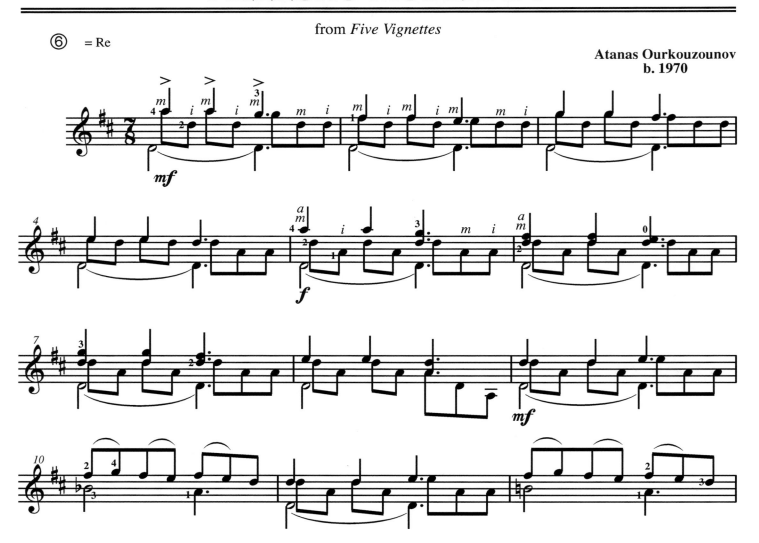

CONTROLLING TEMPO

If you have all other aspects of your technique and musicianship in line, but are lacking a steady sense of pulse, this is a dead giveaway to other musicians that you need more development. Rhythm is a universally recognized weakness of guitarists (and singers), which is particularly noticeable when we play in ensembles. Since we don't get rigorous ensemble training from the early stages, many guitarists get fairly far down the line in a playing career before realizing that they have a problem. Some never acknowledge it, simply saying things like "I'm using rubato;" or, "that's how I *feel* the music."

DON'T USE RUBATO AS AN EXCUSE

I'm not trying to say there isn't room for expression using manipulation of time in music. However, too many guitarists rely on it as the first tool of interpretation, and usually end up corrupting the pulse of the piece. What I would propose is that rubato be the last interpretive tool you add to a piece. The first tools used should be dynamics and articulations.

Before telling yourself "this isn't my problem" and skipping the section, give yourself a little test on a few pieces in your repertoire. First, record yourself playing the piece. Take a little break, let a little time pass before you do the next step. Second, without picking up your guitar, get your score and a pencil. Sing through your piece, marking in where you think there should be rubato as you go. (If you haven't marked rubato before, a common way it is marked is using a forward arrow for speeding up, and a backwards arrow for slowing down. The exact length of the arrow can show exactly where you start to change the tempo and where you achieve a steady tempo.) Finally, listen back to your recording with a metronome in hand. Passages where you have no rubato marked, you should remain fairly true to the metronome. Obviously passages where you have rubato marked, you'll have to temporarily turn the metronome off, or ignore it. While this is not a fail proof test, this will give you an idea of how well your intentions are matching up with your execution.

PULSE OR DEATH (OF THE PERFORMANCE)

For most music, a definite pulse should pervade the majority of the piece. Much Romantic music may have more flexibility; Baroque music tends to be a bit more straightforward, though there is still room to breathe. (These are gross generalizations for which there are numerous exceptions.) All of this becomes a matter of personal taste on some level, of course. But ultimately, there must always be a pulse, something for the audience to hold on to.

> *...develop an inner pulse that you feel as you go through the piece.*

If you've done the above test with one piece and "passed" (in other words, you had moments of rubato where marked, and the rest of the time you had a steady pulse), great. I would recommend trying it with a few pieces from different periods, to confirm that you are able to be purposefully consistent in different types of music. Also, as always, consult with your teacher.

If you realize that you have a problem with this, the cure to the problem is to develop an inner pulse that you feel as you go through the piece. This can take a lot of time, so be patient with yourself. How to do it? Start by forgetting about rubato. You'll be amazed at how much beautiful music you can make using dynamics alone (see section on Crafting Your Interpretation). Use a metronome. This doesn't mean that you can't play expressively – use your dynamics instead of manipulation of time, and I think you'll still feel remarkably satisfied. Play with a metronome exclusively for a week. Then record yourself trying to play the piece with no rubato, using dynamics only. If you do well, then try reinstituting your purposeful use of selective rubato (only what is written in). Continue to check on yourself by recording. When you've strayed too far, go back to the dynamics only approach for a while, with strict use of the metronome.

If you continue to struggle with developing a pulse, simply spend more time with the metronome. You may not like that answer; but it is the only way to truly resolve this problem. As I said before, this does not mean playing without expression - just without rubato. Find the joy in that, and you will eventually discover the pulse in your music.

The music of Bach is some of the most popular music ever written, and requires a great deal of technical skill, as well as a strong sense of pulse. When working on developing your skills, it's always better to start with slightly easier repertoire, and this Allegro by Brescianello is a good place to start working on developing a regular pulse. Use this as an opportunity to practice developing your critical listening skills. In addition to being critical of your pulse, listen for clean arrivals with the left hand; clean attacks with the right hand; even slurs.

STUDY TIPS
- Learn the piece first without the ornaments to ensure that you feel where the principal notes fall.
- The tempo for this piece (like so many others) should be relatively straight, but with breath. Use a metronome to make sure you're not diverging from the pulse.
- Remember that playing with a metronome does not mean playing without dynamics! Use dynamics to bring life to this piece.
- As often happens in modern editions of a work, I have made some changes in an editorial capacity. Some modern editions are very scholarly, and thoroughly explain each change, and show you the original as a reference. Others are more performance oriented, offering the performer's personal solution. Given the scope of this book, I have chosen the latter option, and the changes are not obvious here. You should consult the original score to see what changes I've made, and see if you agree. This is a good exercise in investigation for you! I will tell you that the changes I've made are primarily to write out some of the ornaments that are notated in the original score with less than common symbols (primarily appoggiaturas); I made a couple of changes of duration of voices to account for my opinion on what the tablature was lacking in clarity of notation; and I transposed a few notes up an octave (the original was written for the mandora, an instrument very similar to guitar, but with a 6th string sometimes tuned to G, which lead to a few lines that would not work on a guitar in standard tuning).

ALLEGRO

from *Partita No. IV*

Giuseppe Antonio Brescianello
1690-1758

Once you can trust yourself with a piece such as the Brescianello, Recuerdo triste by Brocá is a good place to try your skills next. In addition to being technically more difficult than the last example (and one of the most challenging pieces in this book), this piece also contains many "obstacles" that must be navigated in terms of tempo and rhythm: one change of time signature, one change of tempo, three fermatas, one section marked *ad libitum*, and a handful of other passages where tasteful rubato is most certainly appropriate. However, there should remain a strong sense of pulse throughout the vast majority of this work.

Ultimately, tempo and rubato are intimately tied in with issues of style (see suggestions under "Discovering the Soul of the Piece.") Each composer and part of world has its own sophisticated sense of rubato. In fact, this is an area where notation is woefully inadequate. Educate yourself about the style, feel the pulse, and then enjoy creating your own rubato.

If this piece is too difficult for you to be able to focus on pulse and rubato, use the Resource section at the end to choose another piece, or consult with your teacher.

STUDY TIPS
- Mark phrases in the score as you go.
- This piece is nothing without dynamics. Great dynamics are even more important than rubato in this piece (as is usually the case).
- Play it relatively straight with great dynamics, and great technical control. Once you can really control what you are doing technically and dynamically, then you can loosen up and add more rubato.
- Measure 10: Enjoy time on both fermatas. Feel a sense of physical calm in these moments. Also, define go-to points in the run – it must have direction. Find the sweet note(s), drive to it, and then relax (ritard) at the end of the run.
- Watch for traps, such as the ornaments in measures 19, 29, 37, as well as the numerous slides; these little ornamentations should not affect the pulse of the passage, which is strong in each of these points. Be sure to practice each passage without the ornament first, to gain a clear idea of the basic rhythmic structure, before adding in the ornament. The ornament in measure 37 is particularly troublesome in that regard, because the material that precedes it does not allow you to begin the ornament before the beat (as most people would do instinctually with the previous two similar ornaments). Experiment with a few ways to resolve this dilemma, and find what suits your musical taste. But remember, the pulse must remain constant.
- Measure 41 is tricky. The fingering I have chosen compromises the duration of the bass note, which should ring longer, and forces an articulation on the bottom line. If you don't like this compromise, experiment with different fingerings to satisfy your musical taste.
- Use your spot practicing skills to help you with difficult passages; pay attention to use of your left hand – good left hand skills will be essential to hitting the many shifts in this piece.
- Rubato is a tool of individual expression, and no one can tell you how or where to do it. But, if you *really* want some pointers, here are a few places where I would most likely do something:
  o Fermatas – in general, most people do way too little on a fermata. Enjoy them more!
  o Measure 13, hold back on beats 1-2, move forward on beat 3, but not too much, just enough to make up for what you held back in beats 1-2. Measure 14 is the "recovery" measure, and by measure 15, make sure you are back at normal tempo, no faster. This same rhythm appears many times throughout the piece, and you could frequently do this kind of rubato. Just be careful not to over use this "trick."
  o Measures 25-26, I would start the run slightly under tempo, sit on the high A (it's a sweet note – use some vibrato!), then push the tempo a bit, and relax at the end of the run.
  o Measure 52, ritard.
  o Measure 65 is marked ad libitum, which is your license to be free – take it! Be sure before you do that you have great technical control on this difficult passage.
  o Ritard at the end of the piece.

Recuerdo Triste

(Sorrowful Remembrance)

José Brocá
1805-1882

35

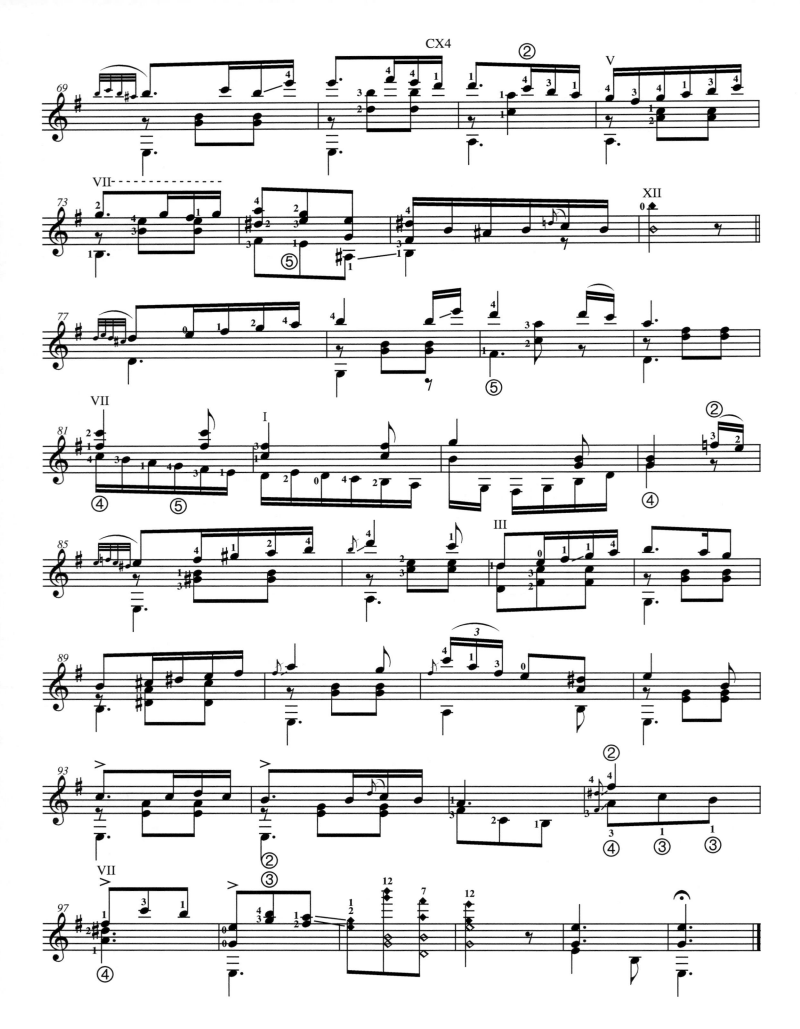

PLAYING *TRULY* LEGATO

This is a tough subject to teach in a book. I've seen plenty of advanced players who are lacking this skill, and have a difficult time hearing it when it is pointed out to them. But we'll give it a try here! I don't want anyone to take this chapter for granted, as this is a critical issue to making beautiful music.

The guitar is one of the most difficult instruments on which to play legato, there are so many things that can go wrong. You can prepare a right-hand finger too early; plant a left-hand finger too early; lift a left-hand finger too early; and the exact synchronization of the hands is critical. Let's deal with each problem individually. To do this, you'll need your Critical listening skills. Don't listen to your playing as you think it sounds; open your ears, and hear what is really happening.

TEST THE RIGHT HAND

To start, try playing alternating i and m on the open first string. Play slowly (no faster than quarter note equals 50 is a good place to start when thinking slow), and listen to whether the notes are truly legato, or if there is a slight break as the next finger is preparing on the string. Many teachers (myself included) work with their students to teach prepared strokes (or planting), and this can be a very useful technique for many reasons. However, in the majority of our playing, we want to play with completely unprepared (or instantaneously prepared) strokes in order to achieve true legato. The more instantaneous your preparation, the more legato your strokes will sound. Play slowly until you are playing fully unprepared strokes before moving on (see the section on The Basics of Good Technique for a review).

TEST THE LEFT HAND

It's impossible to test the left hand alone, as you won't be able to hear the success of your legato connections unless you pluck the string with your right hand. So before moving on to test your left hand, make sure your right hand alone can play as legato as possible. When introducing the left hand, keep it simple. Start by playing just a chromatic scale on the

> *The more instantaneous your preparation, the more legato your strokes will sound.*

first string, frets one through four only. When ascending, be sure not to place any fingers down before the exact moment you need to pluck. When descending, be sure not to lift any fingers before the exact moment you are ready to pluck. Notice if one direction or the other is easier for you. Notice if your right hand is still doing its job. Be very clear and comfortable with doing this on one string, in one position, before complicating things any further.

Once you feel good about the basic function of each hand under these simple tests, try scales that cross a few strings; or try a simple section of one of the pieces in your repertoire, played under tempo. Listen Critically to see if you're able to keep up the legato when things get a bit more complicated. If you want to test your hands at a faster speed, try a little burst – just a short scale, or a very short passage in your piece. If your hands respond well, fantastic. Otherwise, go back to the basics. Like all changes in your playing, if you have work to do here, it won't happen overnight. So be patient; dedicate a portion of your practice time to this every day; and continue to evaluate your progress through recording yourself, using your Critical listening skills, and soliciting the feedback of your teacher and/or other musicians you respect.

To Sum Up: Not everything in music should be legato. But a line should only be broken by musical intention (to create articulations), not by technical limitations. Listen carefully to your playing, and make sure that everything connects (or not) exactly as you intend.

When you're ready to think about legato within the context of a piece, be sure to start simply. This piece by Iannarelli would be a good place to start. The repeated notes give you good opportunity to hear how well the right hand is doing with playing unprepared strokes.

STUDY TIPS
- This piece is relatively simple, but don't underestimate it. Start slowly to hear whether or not you are truly playing legato. I would recommend no faster than quarter note = 44 to start.
- Measure 9-12 (and similar passages), be sure to connect the inner voice.

CANTABILE

from *Cinq études faciles, ou presque...*

Simone Iannarelli
b. 1970

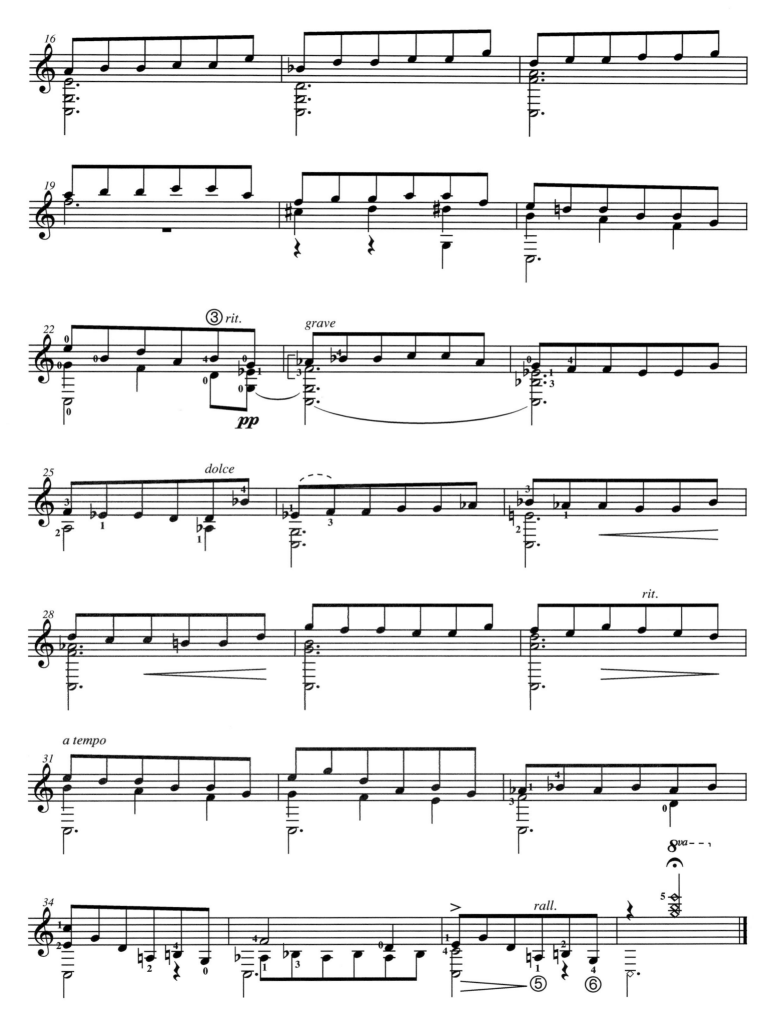

This etude by Napoléon Coste is more complex than it may appear, primarily for how difficult it can be to connect all the lines (not to mention, distinguishing where the lines are). Though the tempo indication is "Agitato," I would recommend playing this very slowly for quite a while, in order for you to be able to hear whether or not you are truly connecting the lines, in all voices. Imagine a violinist playing the line with one bow stroke, as opposed to a stroke for each note; this is the sound you should be striving for.

As you work on this, keep in mind a sense of pulse. The music of Coste has even more room for rubato than some of our previous examples; however, the listener should still be able to understand where the principle beats are.

STUDY TIPS
- Practice very slowly.
- Develop a strong sense of pulse before you begin adding rubato.
- There are lots of string damping issues here (see the section later in the book on this subject for a few pointers). For example, measure 1, beat 1, you must lift the E when you play the C; beat two, you must lift the A when you play the C, but at the same time sustain the bass. And that's just measure 1! Addressing these issues as you learn the piece (as opposed to after) is the simplest way to get it all right.
- Be careful not to roll or break chords unintentionally. Mark every chord that you want to roll, and avoid rolling any others. This is a bad habit of guitarists, and it can affect the pulse of the piece by constantly altering the rhythm. It is a subtle change, but an important one.
- Use dynamics and natural breathing with the phrases from the start; don't worry about more exaggerated rubato until you are more comfortable with the piece.

ETUDE NO. 7

Napoléon Coste
1805-1882

DETERMINING PHRASES AND BREATHING

So once you have most of your basic technical skills under control, we're ready to talk more in depth about making music from the notes that are printed on the page. This doesn't mean that you didn't consider making music up to this point (hopefully you have done that quite a bit already with your teacher), but it is impossible to focus on too many things at once. So now is time for beginning the discussion of phrasing.

SING IT

Before you can work in depth on dynamics or other aspects of interpretation, you have to understand where the phrases of a piece begin and end. Sometimes it is obvious; other times, more confusing. In a piece with a clear melody, the simplest way to determine where the phrases are is to sing it. If it sounds reasonable to take a breath in a certain spot, most likely that is the end of a phrase. There can be phrases of various sizes, very similar to writing prose. You can have an incomplete sentence that still conveys a thought; a complete sentence; a paragraph; a section; a chapter; etc. Similarly, in music, there are phrases of different sizes, which will lead to breaths of different sizes. Be sure to recognize the larger breaths, but don't ignore the smaller breaths. Mark them in your music with a comma. I use smaller commas for smaller phrases; larger commas for larger section breaks.

One of the reasons that singing the piece is so wonderful for determining phrases is that you are forced to physically breathe. When playing the guitar, of course we breathe enough to stay alive. But we are not forced to breathe with any relationship to the music. Not doing so, however, is a mistake.

OVERT BREATHING

One of the biggest lessons I learned in my experiences playing chamber music and studying conducting is the importance of breath in music. In those situations, other musicians are relying on you to convey something about the tempo, the spirit of the music, and your ideas, by using breath. When playing solo guitar, we aren't forced to communicate with anyone to create music – no one needs our breath for a cue, or to respond to our musical ideas. But we should be communicating with the audience – they are the ones from whom we should be aiming to get a response. And overt physical breathing helps the audience better understand your musical intentions. Additionally, **OVERT PHYSICAL BREATHING HELPS YOU TO BETTER UNDERSTAND YOUR OWN INTENTIONS, AND TO EXECUTE THEM MORE FULLY.** Your goal is to truly communicate what you're hearing in your head.

The audience need not hear a loud gasp between each phrase. That would be ridiculous. In fact, maybe they won't *notice* anything at all in terms of your breath. But you should practice taking deep breaths through your mouth at all phrase points. The breaths should reflect the tempo and character of the passage. A fast piece will have quick, probably more audible breaths. A slower piece will have slower, more deliberate breaths.

Frequently, when you begin working on breathing, you'll notice that some body language may begin to enter your playing. When you take a deep breath, the lungs expand, the chest rises, and many players raise the head slightly as well. When you begin to exhale (and play), you may "sink in" to the guitar a bit. Don't fight the natural urge to move a bit when you breathe, and when you play. Don't force it, either. Just relax, and do what comes naturally. If you notice yourself making dramatic changes, solicit feedback from your trusted musical friends. Perhaps it's great, you're playing more relaxed and comfortably now; perhaps you went overboard. Here's also a good opportunity to use video recording to see how you're breathing. If you have a good quality audio recording device, you'll also be able to hear it on the audio recording.

When working on breathing for musical purposes, be sure to always breathe through your mouth (when breathing strictly for relaxation purposes, it's better to breathe in through the nose, and out through the mouth). Trying to take a quick, big breath through your nose can be difficult, and sometimes noisy. Stick to breathing in and out through your mouth. Focusing on breathing will often help with your continued efforts towards playing completely relaxed as well.

I've chosen two very diverse musical examples here to give you a chance to work on identifying phrases and starting to breathe with them. The first piece by Viñas has some phrases that can be seen relatively easily even with an untrained eye – there are rests, double bars, great changes in texture. Those are all visual cues that there may be a breath in the phrase. Go beyond those, and determine the hierarchy of phrasing as you work through this piece.

STUDY TIPS
- This piece is fairly difficult – be sure that you are using your left hand extremely well, and stay under tempo for a long while to ensure that you learn everything with great clarity.
- As with the other pieces, first dynamics, then rubato.
- Watch your rhythm in measures 5-6 and 13-14.
- In measure 18, the melody must sing above the accompanimental chords. I would recommend using rest stroke when possible on the melody.

INTRODUCTION AND ANDANTE

José Viñas
1823-1888

46

The final example for this section is much less visually apparent in terms of the phrasing. There may be a few cues from dynamics and tempo indications, but this piece is all about perpetual motion. You'll have to take your cues primarily from harmonic shifts. A piece such as this can turn into a long, meandering, and meaningless string of notes if you aren't able to bring out the structure of the phrases.

STUDY TIPS

- This piece is also a great arpeggio exercise. Practice the following patterns right hand alone to help you with what you'll need for this piece: pima; amip; paim; pmia.
- It's easy to go faster than the tempo marked in the beginning, but don't be tempted, or you'll regret it when you reach measure 17!
- Measure 19, study right hand alone.
- This piece, as with many others, can be pretty dull without dynamics. Find the high points, and make gradual crescendos/decrescendos to give a beautiful contour, highlighting the harmonic changes.
- Make sure your left hand connects the moving lines (for example, the accented notes in measure 2; the second sixteenth notes in each group measures 8-11; and the half notes on beats 1 and 3 in measure 12). We should hear these as melodies, connected and highlighted from the regular texture of the arpeggio.
- Be sure to mark the main phrases, and plan your dynamics and any rubato (phrase breaths) around these sections. Try to identify the phrases on your own before you read my list (following immediately) of suggested phrases:
  - o Measures 1-6
  - o Measures 7-11
  - o Measures 12-16
  - o Measures 17-22
  - o Measures 23 to end

MEDITANDO

from *Preludios Poeticos*

Jaime M. Zenamon
b. 1953

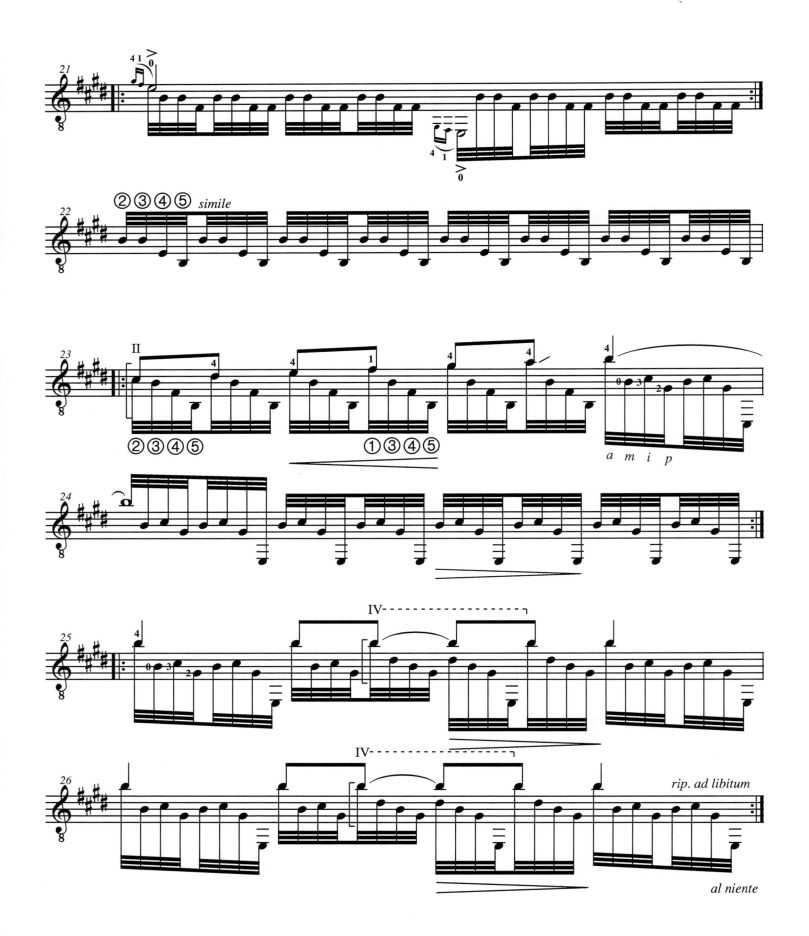

CRAFTING YOUR INTERPRETATION:
DYNAMICS AND COLORS

As classical musicians, most of us don't spend much time improvising music. We read from the page, and interpret the music that others have written. Therefore, our primary goal is to be fantastic interpreters of music. Just as a composer studies other compositions, improvises to find the right ideas, and crafts a well thought out composition, in order to achieve excellence at interpreting music, we need to study interpretive skills, be able to improvise interpretive ideas, and be able to craft a well thought out interpretation.

MYTHICAL MAGICAL MOMENT INTERPRETATIONS
I've often heard from students that they don't want to over-think their interpretations, they prefer to let the music come out as they feel it in the moment. That actually may not sound like a terrible idea, but there are a couple of major problems that can arise from that philosophy. If you haven't spent much time developing your interpretive improvisational skills, what comes out in the moment may not be very successful; or, if you're nervous, your ideas may not come across at all if you haven't given it much thought.

Unless you're prepared to label yourself a master musician with nothing else to learn about musicianship, I recommend that you spend a lot of time on this issue. For me, this is the most entertaining and rewarding aspect of practice, and I hope that if you don't already enjoy this aspect of playing music, you'll come to love it.

START INTERPRETING EARLY
It is never too early to begin thinking about interpretation of a piece. I mean early in two ways: you are never too inexperienced as a player; and the piece is never too fresh. Any player, at any stage of the game, can and should be thinking creatively at all times about interpretation.

Many times in a masterclass, I'll see a student who plays a piece very solidly beginning to end. Well memorized, technically well prepared, but very flat musically. The audience might think, "this person is nervous," or the ultimate musical insult, "this player just isn't very expressive." But what I have fre-

> *Any player, at any stage of the game, can and should be thinking creatively at all times about interpretation.*

quently discovered upon hearing such performances is that neither is the case. Far too often, this technically well prepared performer neglected to even consider musical elements, which is the real cause of the flat delivery. When asked simple questions such as "What is the melody? Can you sing it? Where is the climax?" students frequently can't give a clear answer. Their score is remarkably blank – usually a fairly good indication that little consideration has gone into what to do.

STUDY THE GAME
In sports, people talk about being a "student of the game." This can apply in music as well. An important step to improving your skills as an interpreter is to better understand the "game." There are many different approaches to interpretation, and within those approaches, countless ways to execute the details of the big picture. The more you understand about your likes and dislikes, what is successful and what is not, what is period appropriate and what is not, the more likely you are to be able to convey your ideas to an audience.

How to become a better student of the game? Use your Critical listening skills every time you go to a concert, or listen to a CD. What is the performer doing that you like? That moves you? That you don't like? That you don't understand? That bores you? The more you can specifically identify what it is you like (and don't like) about their interpretations, the more ideas you'll have when you come to the table to work on your own pieces.

KNOW THE SCORE, DISCOVER THE MUSIC

So where to begin in your own playing? Having an understanding of the structure of the piece is important, as is a basic understanding of what the piece is about. So take some time to study the score. The score is our guide, providing us with many important clues as to what the composer is trying to communicate. Begin your dialogue with the composer. You will serve as translator for your audience, so you must first understand the message. What is the title of the piece? What does it mean? What is the form of the piece? Is this a piece with a traditional form (for example, sonata, dance suite, tango) that you should educate yourself about to have a better feel for the spirit of the work? Is there a tempo indication? Did the composer give you any dynamic markings to begin with? Do you understand all of the musical indications? You should take note of all of these clues left by the composer before beginning your own interpretive work with the piece.

In your early readings through the piece, you should discover somewhat naturally the following: Where are the major phrases? Where is the climax? What is the melody? Make sure you can identify all of the above before making any major decisions regarding your interpretation. If you find that you don't discover these things somewhat naturally early on, work to change your perception skills. Make this an important part of what you learn *while* you learn the notes.

IMPROVISE INTERPRETATIONS

Now the real fun begins. A great place to begin your improvising of interpretation is with a simple Sor etude. Sor wrote few musical indications, leaving a fairly blank canvas for us to experiment. The phrases are typically periodic, which makes it very easy to work with small phrases and see how our ideas are working out. Take the first 8 measures of any Sor etude. Can you hear it breaking down further into two four measure phrases? Where would you like to go with the phrase? Think in terms of color and dynamics for now. (In the future, other tools you can use to affect phrasing include rubato, articulations, and vibrato.) Come up with an idea and try it.

How was that? What worked well? Was there anything you didn't like? Now try it a different way. Was that better, worse, or just different? Try at least three different ways to enable yourself to hear it from a different perspective. Feel free to try as many ways as you like! Ultimately, you'll probably come up with one or two interpretations that seem to make the most sense. Write in your ideas (in pencil), and move on to the next eight measure phrase. Apply the same procedure here.

> *For the audience to believe your interpretation, you must commit to it 100%.*

Sometimes as you go through a piece, a decision you make in a new section may change your idea of how a previous section should be interpreted. That's great – that's why we write in pencil! Writing in your ideas shows that thought has been given to what you want to do; likewise, a blank section on your score will show you where you may want to give more thought to your interpretation. Writing it in doesn't mean you can never change it, but leaving it blank is usually in indication of neglect, or lack of commitment. For the audience to believe your interpretation, you must commit to it 100%. There are times I don't agree with a performer's interpretation of a piece. But if they are fully committed to their ideas, I am never bored, and can truly enjoy a performance with an interpretation that would not typically appeal to me.

HAVE NO FEAR

I've noticed that particularly with less experienced students, there is a fear of trying to be expressive. "I have so many other things to think about…What do I know about what sounds good? I'm so inexperienced." If this sounds familiar, get ready to throw your excuses out the window. As for the "so many other things to think about" defense: yes, there are a lot of things to think about when learning to play. However, this doesn't change as you advance – there are always a lot of things to think about! The key is to consider your interpretation separately, before you begin, and to go slowly enough to be able to try your ideas. As for the "what do I know about what sounds good" defense: you know a lot. You've listened to music all of your life, and you most likely have definite ideas about what you like and don't like. Don't be afraid to experiment as a player, and decide what you like and don't like in your own playing. You should listen to other performers as well, and do your best to educate yourself about the origins of the piece you are performing. Of course your opinion counts, but being stylistically informed is important.

In interpreting just as in improvising, there is no right and wrong. There are ideas that sound better than others, but even great musicians can disagree on what sounds "best." Don't be afraid to discover what moves you, and to place a high value on it. The more conviction you feel for your interpretations, the more your audience will believe and truly understand your performance.

This prelude by Tárrega is a wonderful example of a piece that can truly soar when the performer makes phrasing a priority. There are some marks already on the score; but don't stop there. Experiment with many different ideas, and commit fully to your "ideal" interpretation by writing in your musical plan.

STUDY TIPS
- Measure 14 is a surprising harmony, you may want to consider changing color to highlight this interesting moment.
- Don't be too anxious on the fermata in measure 18. Enjoy the moment, use some vibrato, and don't move on too quickly.

Al ilustre Dr. Walter Leckie

PRELUDE No. 5

Francisco Tárrega
1852-1907

MAKING INFORMED FINGERING CHOICES

During one of the last masterclasses in which I played as a student, I learned a very important lesson: the importance of fingerings, and of knowing your musical goal when deciding on fingerings. The class was with a well-known guitarist in Europe. I played Ponce's Thème, varié et finale, which I had been working on for some time. My ideas were clearly defined, I was hoping he would help me convey my ideas more effectively, perhaps give me some fresh perspective on the piece. Fresh perspective delivered! I didn't change my thoughts on this particular piece because of the lesson, but rather gained great insight into what leads musicians to differing opinions on matters of fingerings.

I had fingered the whole piece primarily based on what made the best legato connections. This teacher preferred everything to be fingered based on what made the most interesting or consistent color control. I took the teacher's points into consideration, but when a choice had to be made, to sustain the legato or to sustain color continuity, I still ultimately wanted to choose legato, and he chose color.

WHAT FACTORS CAN MOTIVATE FINGERING CHOICES?

There could be other factors that motivate players to choose a particular fingering. The beginner might choose fingerings that are the easiest, even if they don't allow for legato, continuity of color, or even correct sustaining of note values. The flashy player may like to include a lot of shifts, or a lot of playing in high position to make his job look more difficult! The player who likes simplicity might finger everything in open positions, the player who likes the controlled sound of closed strings might move things up the neck to gain that control. And of course, not all fingerings work for all people – we all have different size hands, different length of fingers, different reach potential.

In the end, I imagine my masterclass teacher still fingers according to color control, and I still finger according to legato. But I learned something. As a teacher, I learned to consider the ideas of the student, and to understand why they have made the choices, both musical and technical, in the work at hand. As a player, I learned that I should keep looking at my playing from different angles. When I can't satisfy multiple agendas with one fingering, I would still choose a fingering that connects the line over one that breaks the line. But perhaps in doing so, I can also make a mental note to change right-hand position slightly at that time, to compensate for the change in color forced by changing strings, as opposed to shifting up the string.

WHAT MOTIVATES YOUR FINGERING CHOICES?

The lesson here is to step outside of yourself. Look at a score you played a while back. Can you identify what motivated your fingering decisions? I know some people (I used to be one of them) who don't write in many fingerings. This is a mistake. Generally, if you haven't written it in, chances are you haven't really considered your options – you are just grabbing whatever feels most natural. This is a great place to start – but may not result in the best musical choices.

> *Perhaps the most important tool we possess as artists is that of awareness.*

So you've found an old piece, and identified your motivations. Now come up with a different motivation. For example, if you were playing everything in the first position when possible, try keeping the melody all on one string. Obviously this may not be a practical solution, but looking from a different angle may allow you to see a new possibility. Force a change in your way of thinking. You might discover something new in the piece that you want to bring out.

You don't have to decide today, in the next week, or in the next month, what motivates your fingering in general. In fact, that can change from piece to piece, and as you grow as a player. Perhaps the most important tool we possess as artists is that of awareness. Simply being aware of what is motivating your decisions is likely to bring about a whole new world of options for you.

Every piece in this book contains fingerings, some more than others, depending on how critical I viewed the passage in question. These fingerings say a lot about my musical ideas.

Notice particularly the right-hand fingerings in the Ourkouzounov; and the left-hand fingerings in measures 71-73 of the Allegro by Brescianello. There are multiple options for each of these passages. The fingerings in the Ourkouzounov show what pattern is most comfortable for my right hand – maybe your right hand would be more comfortable with a different pattern. But if you wish to change it, be sure you can continue the pattern through the rest of the piece – these fingerings were also chosen with consistency in mind. In the Brescianello, I was aiming to keep a consistent slur pattern; however, this fingering compromises consistent tone color, and involves more shifting. This is my choice – what is yours?

As a performer, you should use fingerings in a published score as a starting point, and then feel free to change them to what works well for you. Keep musical considerations at the forefront of your mind as you make any changes.

> *Keep musical considerations at the forefront of your mind as you make any changes.*

This page has been left blank to avoid awkward page turns.

STRING DAMPING

There are countless details in playing music that can affect the overall impression. Once we have our technique in hand, and have developed Critical listening skills, you have the ability to begin to refine the details in your playing. There are as many details as there are notes in a piece.

Have you ever listened to a young pianist who has just discovered the sustain pedal? They are frequently fascinated with the resonance, at the expense of clarity. As guitarists, we have a type of automatic sustain pedal, in that once we play an open string, it sustains until we stop it, or until it decays naturally (this can be a long time on a good instrument!). In addition to this ability, we also have the ability to sustain a fretted note simply by not lifting the left hand. This can be a great thing, allowing us to playing beautiful polyphonic music. But it also can lead to voices "bleeding" into undesired harmonic territory.

ACCIDENTAL DISSONANCE

The issue of bleeding notes is painfully evident when changing harmonies. Good examples of this exist throughout our repertoire, especially any piece in the key of A. There is frequently a lot of back and forth between tonic and dominant, meaning a lot of playing the open fifth and sixth strings. It is very common to hear the return to tonic played as if it were a 6/4 chord, with the dominant ringing in the base. This weakens the return to tonic, and hence the overall musical impact. It's not exactly a dissonance (as can result in other situations), but the harmony is not what the composer intended. So, what to do about it? First, you must teach your thumb how to habitually go after damping those bass notes. This should be done slowly, and out of the context of the piece.

Try this exercise:

First, play an open 5th string; then play open 6th; if you play a rest stroke on the E string, you'll automatically kill the 5th string. That was easy, right? Now it gets a little trickier. Now your low E is ringing, and I want you to play the A again. We want to cut off the E as soon as possible after playing the A, but NOT before – this would create a break in the line, which is an equally grave mistake. So, with the E ringing, we play the A, and the thumb returns immediately to rest upon the 6th string, as if you were going to play it. That's it. The motion should be relaxed and natural, and quick enough that the ear doesn't perceive any bleeding of the E into the new harmony. The two notes are connected, but not perceptibly overlapping.

When you are comfortable with this exercise, try alternating between the 4th and 6th strings. This will force your thumb to do a little string jumping to make the damping possible.

Once that technique is under control, you're ready to see how your new technique can be put to use in the repertoire. In this example by Fernando Sor (Etude, Opus 60, No. 5), first identify the bass notes that will have to be damped, and practice those spots individually. (Hint: several get blocked automatically, three must be purposefully damped.) Then, try reading through it slowly, applying your new skill.

CROSS STRING INTERFERENCE

Another way you can lose clarity in your playing is by allowing the left-hand fingers to sustain notes that should be dead. This is particularly important in counterpoint. Let's consider an example by J.S. Bach. In this passage with two voice counterpoint from the Prelude, Fugue and Allegro, BWV 998, it would be much easier to let certain notes ring while using bars in measures 3 and 4. See if you can identify which notes tend to ring past their notated duration in this passage:

Did you find the notes? The typical problems are: the A on beat 2 of measure 3, the D on beat 3 of measure 3; the E on beat 4 of measure 3; the C# on beat 1 of measure 4; the F# on beat 2 of measure 4; and the B on beat 4 of measure 4. Six notes in two measures that we need to be aware of! This is one of the reasons playing the music of Bach is so difficult. How to stop each note? In order: I would stop the A by lifting the half bar at the end of beat two; stop the D by lifting the finger; stop the open E by blocking it gently with the left finger preparing to play the next note; stop the C# by hinging off the bar (leave the tip of the finger on the A to sustain it for the full beat); stop the F# by blocking it gently with the left finger preparing to play the next note; stop the B with the "i" finger, which also serves as preparation for the first note of the next measure.

MELODIC LINES VERSUS ARPEGGIOS

Sometimes, we sustain notes because we aren't clear what is a scalar passage (or simply a melodic line), and what is an arpeggio. There are great examples of this in many of Bach's works, for example this passage from the BWV 1001 fugue.

59

This passage alone could be the subject of an entire chapter. This is a good place to look once you have a grasp of the concept. I put it here to illustrate the complexity of the issue. For our purposes, let's start with a clearer example, an excerpt from The Czech Fairy Tales by Stepan Rak.

In this excerpt, the first two measures indicate quarter notes, meaning each note would only last one beat. I think many guitarists would interpret this passage thinking of it as an arpeggio, allowing the bass note to ring as long as the harmony is constant. So the D on beat one would hold the length of a half note (while playing beat two as a separate voice), and then the D would be stopped immediately after playing the A on beat three. The bass note A on beat three would last while you play beat four, and be stopped immediately after you play the downbeat of measure two. This is a way of interpreting the written notation, which could certainly be subject to discussion. However, what definitely should NOT happen is for the D on beat one of the first measure to ring throughout the entire measure! You must decide at what point you want to stop it: either literally according to the score, or musically according to the harmonies. In measure four, beat 1, be sure to stop the open E after you play the next note on the second string – this should sound like a line, not an arpeggio.

> ### *What you have to avoid is the tendency to let notes bleed into changing harmonies simply because the technique of the instrument makes it difficult not to.*

Composers don't always write that all of the notes of an arpeggio are to be sustained, but it is a natural musical tendency. For example, in measure three of the Sor etude above, most people would let those notes ring over one another instead of playing them literally as eighth notes. Why? Because they form a chord, whereas the previous measure was scalar movement. What you have to avoid is the tendency to let notes bleed into changing harmonies simply because the technique of the instrument makes it difficult not to. You should listen instead to what the music is trying to tell you. It is easier not to let go of notes that you've already fretted with the left hand, and not to block them with the right hand – both of these require action. So unless you take the time to think about these issues, your listeners may be left a bit confused about where the melody is going, or what exactly is the harmony. When you hear a great piece played with all the right notes, it sounds very nice. But when you hear a great piece played with all the right notes AND with this level of detail, the genius of both the piece and the performer shines through.

Some of these cases of bleeding notes are more difficult to spot than others. But if you slow down, and really listen to what is sounding at any given time, you'll find the spots. Then to fix them, each case requires a different solution. Sometimes, you have to lift a finger; sometimes, you have to use another finger (left or right hand) to stop the string; sometimes, you have to refinger the whole passage to make it work in a manner that makes musical as well as technical sense.

SYMPATHETIC VIBRATIONS

On an even deeper level, the guitar has a lot of really beautiful sympathetic vibrations. However, these vibrations can also interfere with the power of a change in harmony. There are times when we have to pay attention to stopping the vibration of strings that we haven't even played! But the power of a single note or a clear chord is worth the effort. Listen for these in your playing, and get creative in finding ways to stop those errant sounds. My favorite technique to stop sympathetic vibrating in the basses is to plant my thumb on the fourth string and just roll it back quickly to touch the fifth and sixth strings (assuming you don't want any of those strings to ring). Again, I would practice this technique outside of your repertoire to get used to it.

String damping is an issue of a high level of detail, and an issue of great importance. Details are what make the difference between good players and great players. If you're ready to take the next step, slow down, and open your ears. You may be surprised at what you hear.

Try your hand with your new damping skills on this Bolero by Arcas. The obvious notes that require damping (hopefully they are obvious at this point!) are the bass notes, the frequent alternation between the 5th and 6th strings. If your ear is starting to listen Critically, you may also notice in the first two beats, you have a decision to make about how long to hold the notes of the a minor arpeggio. Do all those notes last for the entire first two beats? Are you going to interpret the given note values literally, requiring quite a lot of damping? Or might you let them ring until you play the E on beat 2 1/2 , and then stop everything except that E, and the bass note? This is a very common dilemma that arises in guitar writing. Each player must decide for himself! Keep an eye out for dilemmas such as this throughout the piece.

STUDY TIPS
- Bass note damping!
- In measure 18, there is a large shift from the chord on the downbeat up to the next note. The Cs in the chord are automatically cut as you have to let them go; the first string is automatically cut by preparation for the next note; but watch out for that third string, that must be damped (I use p to damp it).

BOLERO

Julián Arcas
1832-1882

ARTICULATIONS

Once you've got control over what strings ring when, it will be a simpler task to consider articulations. If you are technically able to control errant strings, and musically able to perceive them, the next step is to actively decide on a plan for articulations. In a lyrical piece, your decision may be simple – play everything legato. In an imitative piece, you may have many options to consider in terms of which notes could be staccato, which legato.

EXPERIMENT WITH IDEAS, CREATE A PLAN

One of my favorite places to consider options for articulations is in the fugue subjects of J.S. Bach. There is plenty of material here, much of which can be (and has been) interpreted successfully with a wide array of possibilities for articulations. Experimenting with a few subjects will help you develop your skill at looking for alternate solutions; and ultimately at determining your general taste for articulations.

Try this subject from the fughetta in Bach's BVW 996, with three different articulation plans:

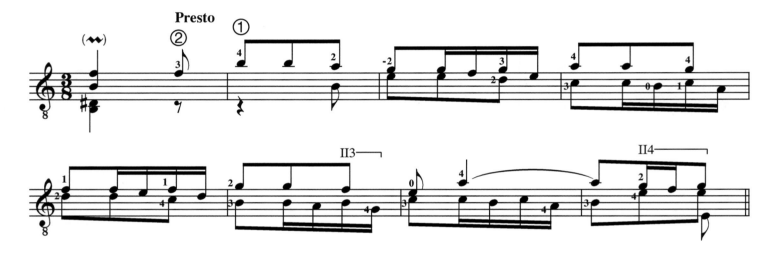

Try playing the subject alone (without the other voices) to determine what articulation plan you like best. Then try with other voices, and see what is practical in terms of execution when other voices are added. Sometimes we must make decisions (to compromise a choice in articulation) when complexity won't allow us to do the same articulation plan when playing multiple voices. Generally, it is best not to compromise the consistency of the articulation in various appearances of the same motive/theme. If you cannot carryout your articulation plan in every appearance of the motive, first, reconsider your fingerings to see if there is any other way to play the passage and carry out all your musical intentions. If not, you may wish to consider an alternate articulation plan that allows you to be consistent in all appearances of the motive.

> *...be sure that you are consistent with how you apply articulations in ideas that recur within any piece of music.*

This concept applies not only to fugue subjects and imitative passages, but also to accompanimental chords in waltzes, and other recurring melodic or harmonic passages in any piece of music. There are choices to be made regarding articulation in virtually every piece of music in your repertoire – look back at some of your recent pieces to see how attentive you are to this subject. If you have not adequately considered your options, experiment with other ways to articulate and bring life to phrases you already know so well. Primarily, be sure that you are consistent with how you apply articulations in ideas that recur within any piece of music.

CURE ACCIDENTAL ACCENTS

Notice what happens when you play a note staccato. Occasionally, that note is accented, as sometimes we tend to play staccato notes also accented. When done intentionally, this can be a great effect. Be careful not to do it unintentionally. The opposite can also be true: that the first note after the staccato note or passage is accented; and not necessarily because we play it louder; but rather, our ear perceives it as more important, since the note lasts longer. Beware of these two phenomenons, and be sure to use them to your advantage as best suits the particular passage you are studying.

To sum up, many players use of a variety of articulations in Baroque music. I've found that, for my taste, not enough students use variety of articulation in Classical music. This really helps to bring to life some of those simpler pieces from the period that are often labeled "boring." Next time you are ready to doom a piece to the boring list, do your part to see what interesting motives you can discover/uncover/create by using articulations.

Try this Capriccio by Brescianello. You can play it all legato, and it sounds nice. You can add a few articulations here and there in either voice, and liven it up a bit. You can also use articulations as a means of ornamentation on the repeats. Be creative!

STUDY TIPS
- Watch the rhythm in measures 19. Practice with a metronome to make sure that you keep the same pulse when you switch to triplets.
- Note the rhythm of the melody in measure 5. Compare that with how the melody is written in measures 21 and 23. Measure 5 is a perfect example of how notation can help you understand which voice is melody, and which is accompaniment. I would recommend that you treat the melody with the same rhythm in measures 21 and 23 (meaning sustain the melody note on beat one while you play the next two eighth notes). This is subjective, and a change from the original score, but to my ear, this is the correct solution. In the first piece by Brescianello that is is included in this book, I made this kind of alteration in the course of my editing. Here, I'm leaving it to you. Use your ears to determine where the voices are, what should sustain, and where to add articulations.

CAPRICCIO

from *Partita No. X*

Giuseppe Antonio Brescianello
1690-1758

USING VIBRATO

Guitar is the only instrument which is capable of truly carrying multiple voices, and also capable of playing with vibrato. Bowed string instruments and singers, who frequently seem to be incapable of playing/singing without vibrato, can't truly carry multiple voices. Piano, organ and harp, which carry multiple voices, can't do vibrato. So we are, yet again, uniquely capable on our instrument!

USE VIBRATO DELIBERATELY AND CONSISTENTLY

What makes vibrato so difficult for us is that we are frequently so "busy" when playing the guitar, that we are not able to be consistent in our use of it. A singer doesn't come in and out of vibrato in the middle of a phrase – they either use it or they don't, depending on the style. True, faster note values have less vibrato; but if the violin is playing sustained notes while the piano is busy with the accompaniment, the violin continues the vibrato throughout the entire phrase.

When we play all voices on the guitar, we are sometimes incapable of maintaining vibrato in a melodic section, due to the complications of playing the accompaniment at the same time. The left hand simply can't do it all.

So we as guitarists have come to learn to love the one "special" note or chord that gets the vibrato; the moment in the piece where we can relish our gift. Perhaps that is what separates us from the pianists, organists and harpists, and we should embrace it. My word of caution: just be careful not to use vibrato every chance you get – you'll likely end up with a very confusing message to the audience (especially any non-guitarists who don't understand why you don't continue with that beautiful idea). Always consider the musical context and make sure the vibrato adds to the beauty, and doesn't stand out in a way that makes the rest of the melody pale in comparison.

PRACTICE VIBRATO AS A TECHNIQUE

A few technical words of advice on achieving a relaxed vibrato. To make vibrato, you have to push and pull the string. It should be a relaxed motion, not a tense one. You shouldn't squeeze harder with the left hand, or grimace; neither of these things will help! Use your large muscle groups, and keep your finger tip on a fixed point (don't let it slide on the string).

> *Always consider the musical context and make sure the vibrato adds to the beauty.*

Start by choosing a particularly responsive note (I like the fourth string, seventh fret), and a strong finger (usually 2). Leave your thumb planted lightly on the back of the neck, but do not apply pressure. Start slowly by allowing your hand to move side to side, each side of your hand alternately touching the neck of the guitar in a steady rhythm. This is a slightly exaggerated motion, but is great for training the direction of the motion. While you're doing this, make sure the rest of your hand and body stays completely relaxed. The path your hand follows should draw a semi-circle from the neck. Attempts to "force" the vibrato generally cause your hand to move in parallel motion to the neck – this won't work comfortably in context.

After you've developed a slow comfortable vibrato with a good arcing motion, gradually speed up the pace. Some people like to practice vibrato with a metronome, gradually increasing the speed, or the number of vibrations per click. This can be a useful tool for you to experience the different sensations possible in vibrato. In the end, it has to feel natural.

Experiment with vibrato on different notes in different ranges of the instrument. Hear how a faster vibrato sounds on higher notes; and a slower vibrato sounds in the lower register. The speed of your vibrato can be affected by the style of music you are playing, and the intensity you wish to create in that moment. The better you understand the range of possible sounds and how to achieve them, the more successful you will be at incorporating your musically desired vibrato in your performance, beyond what comes naturally for the hand.

This Berceuse by Coste is a wonderful place to develop your vibrato. It has quite a bit of shifting, so be sure you are confident in how your left hand moves before you try adding the vibrato. The quarter note melodic chords are begging for vibrato, but you most likely won't have much time to get in vibrato on the eighth notes. This is a good opportunity to figure out where it works and where it doesn't.

STUDY TIPS
- Open string fingerings and faster note values force you to balance your use of vibrato. Don't over use vibrato on a melody note that is immediately preceded or followed by an open string. You may also carefully consider alternate fingerings to allow for more use of vibrato.
- Measure 25 has a short scale which should not present too much difficulty, but you need to think about your right-hand fingering. Many students would start a scale like this with the thumb since it starts on a bass string. However, it's really too quick to use the thumb successfully for the entire scale; and switching from thumb to fingers in the middle of a passage is not usually the best solution. I'd strongly recommend playing the entire scale with i and m.
- Take a look at the form of the piece before you start playing. It is a short rondo, meaning the theme (measures 1-8) appears in alternation with subsequent sections. Every time you see "D.C.," return to the beginning and play the main theme; then proceed to the next section you have not yet played.

BERCEUSE

Oeuvre inédite

Napoléon Coste
1805-1882

DISCOVERING THE SOUL OF THE PIECE

When you've gained control of your technique, developed your listening skills, and worked on expanding the set of interpretive tools at your disposal, what's left? One of the most critical aspects of playing music is to get to the heart of the piece you are playing. To find its soul, and to unite it with your soul, your sense of style.

The key is to represent the spirit of the piece, being mindful of both the composer's intentions and your perspective. For some, this is the sole reason for playing music, and they are caught up in chasing this idea from the start. Other players get a bit caught up in the many technical demands of our instrument, and they have missed the point on this important aspect of playing music.

Both types of players can run into problems with the ultimate goal of finding the soul of the piece, and both can benefit from some of the same types of work. Players who are obsessed with playing with feeling sometimes ignore the intentions of the composer and the style appropriate to the period in their quest, resulting in a passionate, yet possibly inappropriate (indeed sometimes strange) performance. Players who get hung up with the technical side of playing may be very accurate, but a bit dry to listen to.

LISTEN TO THE GREAT INTERPRETERS

Whether you're naturally expressive or naturally technical, I would recommend listening to recordings of great players who are known for their interpretations in a certain period. Listen to recordings not only by guitarists, but by pianists, singers, violinists, etc. Within each period, there will inevitably be different interpretations, and only you can decide what you like best. But ultimately, you'll begin to notice things that simply are not done in a certain style period. And maybe there's a reason for that. Or things that everyone does in a certain style….again, there's likely a reason for that.

KNOW YOUR HISTORY

Another way to augment your understanding of the period is to really know your music history. If you've studied music in college, you've likely had classes that did a pretty good job of covering basic information. Review your books. If you've not studied music history in school, try registering for a music history class at a local college.

> *...you are responsible for interpreting a work of art, for bringing to life notes that were conceived by someone else.*

For specific information on interpreting certain periods, there are a number of authoritative books out that that may help. Do a search at your library to see what resources you can find that may help you better understand aspects of performance practice (for example, ornamentation; articulation; phrasing) that may guide your interpretation. See also the recommendations in the Resources section.

You should also research the composer of any work you are playing, to understand about where they are coming from. If you learn about stylistic ideas in the classical period, that's great. But even better if you understand, for example, some of the differences in essence between the music of Giuliani and Sor. This comes from doing your homework on the specific composers, beyond the style period.

Finally, you should have a thorough understanding of the form of the piece – a sonata, a suite (and each movement within it), a waltz, a milonga, etc, all have very distinct style traits that you should be Critically aware of, and be looking for the markers in the piece. Understanding the form will help guide your interpretation. Something as simple as looking it up in *The New Harvard Dictionary of Music* (if you don't already own a copy, order one today - it's an indispensable resource) can go a long way towards your understanding of basic form.

DON'T LET YOUR KNOWLEDGE CLOG YOUR PROCESS

With all of this information, it's easy to again get bogged down with over thinking how you "should" play a piece. The information you learn about a composer, a genre, what was going on at the time the piece was written....all this should help inform your interpretation, but not clog your process. In the end, you are responsible for interpreting a work of art, for bringing to life notes that were conceived by someone else. That's why it must be a true union of your musical soul, and of the piece. Do some soul searching. Experiment with all your interpretive tools. Decide which ones are appropriate for the piece. Don't be afraid to try new things, and expose yourself to raw emotions. That's where all the music lies.

This piece by Casséus is a beautiful work with a deep soul. It presents few real technical challenges, but you must get the groove of this piece in order for it to really work.

STUDY TIPS
- Most important for this piece is that you find the rhythmic groove. Practice the piece consistently with a metronome, and then turn it off and make sure you can feel the groove of the rhythm as you play.
- Take special care with the rhythm in measure 7.
- Look up some information about the composer and about the merengue to help color your interpretation.
- Enjoy the syncopation!

Merengue

Frantz Casséus
1915-1993

This book is all about trying to get you to slow down, listen, and choose repertoire that might be a bit easier than your normal pieces in order to allow you to grow. The piece I've chosen to highlight here is a bit more difficult than most other pieces in this book, but likely is still easier than some of the pieces that you've studied in the past! If it is too difficult for you, find another piece from the list of suggestions to work on instead (see the Resources section at the end of the book).

I couldn't resist choosing this beautiful piece by Sergio Assad. It's a great piece to work on the many different topics we've covered in this book. Though technically it presents only modest challenges, musically, it is exceptionally revealing. You'll need to find the soul of the piece in the breath of the phrases; in your tone production; in your dynamic shaping; in your touch; in every little detail of this piece.

STUDY TIPS
- This piece must breathe, so sing through it, and mark phrases as you go.
- There are no dynamic indications; it is an open invitation for the performer to discover his or her own plan. Be sure to experiment with different ideas, identify climactic moments, unexpected moments, tender moments, and capture all of these (and more) in your interpretive plan. Write it in using pencil, and don't be afraid to adjust as you go.
- One of the greatest challenges of this piece is keeping the melody legato. Don't let your ear ignore breaks in the line that are caused by challenging passages, or places where it's simply easy not to play legato. (The first trap comes in measure 1- don't place your bar too early, or you'll cut the very first melody note, getting off to a rough start!)
- While working to connect the melody in the top voice in measure 1, you'll also have to pay attention to the counterpoint in the middle voice. You're immediately challenged with a note that wants to bleed into the next note (the c# into the b). This is a line, and the notes should not ring like and arpeggio. However, later in the piece, there are passages that are written as eighths, but really should ring as arpeggios (for example, the beautiful harmonies in measure 19). It's your job to sort out what should ring as an arpeggio, and what is a melodic figure that should not bleed. Use your critical listening skills to sort one from the other.
- In measure 10, be careful not to release the bar when reaching for the d on the fourth string.
- I have left all fingerings on this piece as the composer originally indicated. However, in measure 24, I would recommend considering an alternative here. I would recommend that you play the last note of the measure (the d) on the second string with your fourth finger. By doing this, you sacrifice a bit of the bass by shifting early; but it makes it much easier to connect that pickup note with the downbeat of the next measure. It's a choice each player will have to make for him/herself.
- Bring attention to the melody notes in the bass from the very first pick up note on beat 3 of measure 26.
- In measure 35, don't rush the sixteenth notes in this (or subsequent) measure(s). Playing them strictly in time, or perhaps even with a bit of rubato working in your favor (with a slight pulling back on the first note or two of the group), will make these passages manageable.

VALSEANA

Sergio Assad
b. 1950

Improving Your Sight-Reading

This could be (and has been) the subject of a book all by itself, but we should at least cover some basic ideas about reading here. Guitarists are notoriously poor sight-readers. To be fair to us, we have a more difficult task at hand than most other instruments: in addition to playing multiple notes at a time, we also have the obstacle/opportunity to play those notes in a variety of places. Having options is wonderful when we have time to consider them; but on first sight, this provides us with a unique challenge that no other instrument faces. Enough defending ourselves…on to how to improve your skills.

> *Good sight-reading skills will make it more fun to read through repertoire, make it easier to learn new pieces, and, if you're a working musician, will open doors for you in the professional world.*

Know Where the Notes Are

First, you must be confident in your fretboard knowledge. In my undergraduate days at Peabody, we had a class called "Guitar Skills," that I recall as being painful, yet important. The objectives of this class were great and varied (theory, sight-reading, fretboard knowledge, and more), but this was my first realization that after playing the guitar for more than a decade (at that point), I still didn't have a thorough knowledge of the fretboard. If this is you, there is some work you can do to improve in this area.

One of my favorite exercises is one that I use with my students to test their knowledge of the fretboard. Try playing all notes of a given pitch, in all locations on the fretboard (being reasonable – up through the 14th fret on string 3-6, and 18th fret on strings 1-2). Start with the lowest pitch, and play all the unisons and octaves, working your way up the strings. Use a metronome to keep you steady. Start slowly, as slowly as you need to be able to do it accurately at a consistent tempo.

You can go crazy with ways to test your knowledge; this is just one way that I've found to be not too intimidating and yet productive. If you can't do this with ease, you've got some studying to do.

Pre-Read; Play Slowly; Get the Main Idea; Read Ahead

If you have good fretboard knowledge, your sight-reading should be stronger than without it. But we can all use improvement in this area. See the Resources section for a few suggestions on books that may help you with your sight-reading (I particularly recommend following one of the methods that feels appropriate for your level, in addition to daily reading of repertoire). A few pointers you may want to consider:

1. Always "pre-read" the piece before beginning to play. Look at the form (are there any repeats? da capos? where does it end?); the tempo indication; the time and key signatures; any changes in time/key signature throughout the piece; the fastest note value (this will help you in determining your tempo); tricky rhythms, shifts, or chords; anything else that could catch you off-guard if you came upon it suddenly. These are the kinds of things I'm looking for when I "pre-read" a piece.

2. Play at a conservative tempo. It should still make musical sense, but don't try to hit the tempo marked on the page on first sight.
3. Go for the "idea" of the piece instead of perfection. In other words, don't get hung up if you miss a note or make a mistake. The most important aspect in this phase of playing is to maintain continuity. If you're crashing and burning, then either you need to start again slower, or play a piece that is easier, or both. But generally, when sight-reading, if you miss a note here and there but keep the rhythm steady, you (and your audience, if you're sight-reading on a gig) will forget the mistake by the next measure and be able to focus on the overall impression of the piece. This is NOT permission to practice your pieces this way – this advice only applies to sight-reading!
4. Training the eyes (and mind) to read ahead is critical. Without this, you will never achieve fluency in sight-reading. Don't look at what you're doing- look at where you're going. Just as when you're driving, the faster you drive, the further ahead you look. The same principle applies to reading music. If you can't do it, you need to play slower, to allow your brain to always be one step ahead of your fingers.

Good sight-reading skills will make it more fun to read through repertoire, make it easier to learn new pieces, and, if you're a working musician, will open doors for you in the professional world. Spend a few minutes each day consciously developing your skills in this area – you'll be glad you did.

COPING WITH PERFORMANCE ANXIETY

It sounds like an oversimplification, but truly, the best antidote for performance anxiety is solid preparation. If you know that you are able to perform the piece(s) well, and have a history of doing so in the practice room, you've removed a powerful cause of anxiety – the fear (or knowledge) that you may not be able to "pull it off" in concert. If you're well prepared, you know it is *possible* to do it.

There are still a number of obstacles that can make performing difficult, uncomfortable, or downright terrifying. Some people suffer from physical symptoms of nerves, such as sweaty palms or shaking hands. Others suffer from mental symptoms, such as fear of mistakes, fear of memory lapses, or fear of the audience.

PHYSICAL EFFECTS OF ANXIETY

Shaking hands and sweaty fingers can certainly get in the way of your ability to perform as you have practiced. One of the most effective means of dealing with physical symptoms that I've witnessed is to simply mentally accept the symptoms, to expect and allow them to happen. This may seem a bit backwards. But what choice do you have? Your hands are shaking; your palms are sweating. By simply permitting them to do it, you remove your anxiety over that aspect. Frequently, this, combined with good preparation and experience, eventually leads to the disappearance of the physical manifestations of anxiety. Don't expect your hands to stop shaking overnight. Rather, accept that they will shake, and move on with it. If it gets better in a few years, fantastic. If not, you'll have learned not to be mentally or emotionally phased by a little tremble. Don't allow the physical effects to cause you emotional symptoms as well.

MENTAL EFFECTS OF ANXIETY

In order to feel relaxed while performing, it is helpful to try to discover the roots of your anxiety. When I was a child, I never felt nervous performing. It wasn't until I entered college that I started to have anxiety. The power of the knowledge (knowing exactly what I was doing wrong) overwhelmed my ability to enjoy the performance. I also came to realize that I wasn't fully prepared.

The first step for me was to begin to be fully prepared (along the lines of the in depth understanding of music that we have talked about in this book). That took a few years. Then the next step was to learn to trust it, and regain the same spirit that I had in my playing when I was a child. That took many more years, and in some ways, I think will always be a work in progress. There is always a little part of me that says "Are you sure you practiced enough? Are you sure you're good enough? Are you sure you know this piece?" The good thing is, when I've done my work, I know the answer is yes (instead of "maybe"). And with every concert I play, the greater my experience and confidence becomes. The more I'm able to relax and trust my work in the practice room, the more the music is able to come through to the audience. And that's why we perform.

> *...it is helpful to try to discover the roots of your anxiety.*

So how to get to a point of comfort? For me, it took a few teachers along the way, first to train me to practice well, then to pat me on the back and reassure me that I was worthy of making music, and to help me relax. All through that path, I sought out performing opportunities appropriate to my level, and as many of them as I could schedule.

One truth I discovered as I completed my masters degree, was that any "high pressure" concert (such as a degree recital) went immeasurably better if I had scheduled a handful of "warm-up" concerts. So I started seeking out opportunities to play in retirement homes or churches, often for no or very low pay, as a means of trying out the program for a friendly audience. When I did this, my anxiety was greatly reduced on the day of the "pressure" concert. I had worked out some of my nerves on audiences where I didn't have as much fear of criticism or the result of the concert. I keep this method today. When I'm trying out new repertoire, I don't do it at a high-pressure concert (a New York debut, a GFA convention, etc.). I'll try it out first as many times as possible in lower pressure settings.

...what helps cure anxiety more than anything: solid preparation, a positive attitude, and experience.

Finally, I'd recommend reading books on the subject of performing. You never know which book might have the one sentence that changes your mental perspective, and unlocks your ability to achieve your real potential in performance. See the Resources section for ideas on books to read.

BE PREPARED; BE POSITIVE; KEEP PERFORMING

In the end, what helps cure anxiety more than anything: solid preparation, a positive attitude, and experience. The more opportunities you have to perform, the better. Guitar societies often have monthly meetings where students can perform; try your church; local retirement center; your next family gathering; a group of fellow students in a performance class; whatever opportunity comes up, take it (as long as you're well prepared – never set yourself up for failure by being unprepared!) The more opportunities you give yourself to overcome your fears and build positive experiences, the sooner you'll feel confident performing. Remember why you do this, why you play the guitar – most likely it has nothing to do with fear and anxiety! Remember the things you love about music before you go on stage, and strive to share that with your audience.

Insightful teaching is invaluable, both in your hired teacher, and in your own self evaluation.

What does it take to be able to play more advanced music well? Quality practice; attention to details; and time, both in terms of hours per day, and in terms of years experience. The best players are the best students. One of the goals of this book is to develop your Critical listening skills to allow yourself to accurately evaluate your own playing – to become your own best teacher. As I stated in the introduction, you may see a teacher one day a week for an hour. A dedicated student puts in six more days of practice each week, often several hours each day. If you aren't skilled enough to "teach" yourself during those hours, your time is being used very inefficiently. Insightful teaching is invaluable, both in your hired teacher, and in your own self evaluation.

Go listen to concerts; read magazines and books about guitar. Attend local and international festivals and conventions. Become a member of your local guitar society, and of the Guitar Foundation of America. Don't miss an opportunity to learn more about the guitar, and become connected with others who do what you do.

Those who are looking at a career in music often ask, what does it take to "make it" in music? Since entering school, I've seen very talented players leave the business; I've seen less naturally gifted players excel and rise to the top of their generation in various aspects of music. "Making it" in music can mean many different things; and the ability to make it depends on many aspects of your personality.

WHAT IS YOUR DEFINITION OF SUCCESS?
Students without ambition of making a career out of the classical guitar may define success in terms of their playing goals: success is to be able to play in control; to be able to play pieces at a certain level of difficulty; or to be able to perform confidently in public. If this is you, then the work you're doing by using this book will help you get there. Be honest with yourself; seek the best instruction possible; supplement your regular instruction by attending masterclasses and festivals. Work diligently and intelligently to achieve your goals.

IF YOU WANT TO BE A PROFESSIONAL...
Those who intend on a career in classical guitar can also have various definitions of success. Some would define success as simply earning a living playing and teaching music. Others would define it as nothing less than classical guitar stardom. It is the latter group who tend to fade out the quickest, realizing that, indeed, there are few who become superstars in our very competitive world, and achieving that status involves not only hard work and sacrifice (both financial and emotional), but also good fortune.

The work you're doing by using this book is important for you as well; but to make a career of it, you have to do more than just play the guitar. You have to also succeed at the business end of music. If you're in the first category of aspiring professionals (or somewhere in between that and superstardom), there are many opportunities for earning a living as a classical guitarist in addition to (or besides) the dream that many have of being a concert guitarist. You can teach children in your home or at a studio, either independently or using one of the systems of teaching that are currently successful (such as Suzuki or Childbloom). You can teach adults, in your home, music shops, community colleges, evening adult extension classes, or universities. You can get your teaching credential and teach in one of the many counties across the US that are starting to support guitar programs in public schools. You can play background gigs for private events, booking them on your own or using an agent. You can arrange concerts for local groups such as community colleges, churches and retirement centers, all of which may be able to offer small fees if you find the right places. All of these opportunities expand when you begin to get involved with chamber music.

I'm a firm believer in the fact that if you truly love music and can't see your life without it, you will be able to earn a living in music. You may never be rich or famous; but if you're willing to work hard, almost anyone can have a career teaching and playing the guitar.

THEY HAVE TO KNOW YOU TO HIRE YOU

For those whose desire is to make it to the concert artist level, a few further pointers (many of which are helpful to all guitarists, regardless of your aspirations). First, I think it is important to immerse yourself in the world of guitar. Follow all the advice above, plus, realize the importance of networking. Networking is an invaluable part of "making it." No one will ever invite you to perform if they've never heard of you. So get out and meet people, and without high expectations. Just get to know the people in the world of guitar. Once you've earned their respect (which takes time), the invitations will begin to come in. Have patience, and be respectfully persistent.

DON'T WAIT FOR THE PHONE TO RING

Be professional and be proactive. Create a press kit, demo CD, and a website. Contact everyone you're able to reach who hires people doing what you do. Respond quickly to all phone and email messages. Be polite and easy to work with, and you'll have a better chance at getting a return invitation.

COMPETE TO BE HEARD

Competitions can be a great way to get people to hear you, especially if you're lucky enough to make the final round in a major international competition. Winning isn't everything....you just have to be heard.

Most importantly, have a healthy attitude about competitions. At the end of the day, the results of any competition come down to a matter of personal taste, and you can't change yourself to cater to a jury (nor should you try).

You can (and should) always represent yourself well. Be prepared. Select your repertoire thoughtfully to show diversity, but also show your strengths. Avoid things like Bach (which everyone has their own very well defined opinion about), and other warhorses which can either greatly divide or tire out a jury. Choose pieces that suit you well, that you feel strongly about, and pieces with which you have something unique to say.

> *...immerse yourself in the world of guitar.*

If you do all this, and perform well, you should hold your head high, regardless of the result. Though it can be frustrating not to get the result you were hoping for, no one likes a sore loser. And most people don't want to hire a sore loser! So instead of getting angry, or getting down on yourself, see if there's anything you can learn from the situation to improve for the future. If you delivered your best and still didn't win, maybe you need to adjust your repertoire; maybe you just have some growing to do; or maybe you just need to get the right jury that has the same taste as you. Don't give up; keep a healthy attitude; and use competitions as an incredible learning experience, both in your preparation, and the time at the actual event.

REACHING THE NEXT LEVEL

The point of this book has been to try to help devoted players reach the next level in their playing, whatever that may be at this point. Eventually, with dedication to the quality and the details in your playing, your step-by-step progress will lead you to realize your full potential.

A few reminders of what I consider the keys to reaching the next level:

- **Slow down!**
- **Listen critically. Pay attention to details.**
- **Identify and address your obstacles, both technical and musical.**
- **Play pieces that are technically within your reach; and occasionally pieces that are even "easy" for you.**
- **Don't let your technique get out of control as you strive for more difficult repertoire.**
- **Always think about making music, not just playing the notes.**

When you identify and address your obstacles, you'll reach the next level in your playing.

None of us are ever done learning about music. Keep an open mind about your playing; reward yourself for your progress; and enjoy the journey.

When you identify and address your obstacles, you'll reach the next level in your playing.

SELECTED ANNOTATED BIBLIOGRAPHY

By no means is the following list comprehensive, and I mean no disrespect to any publications that are not on this list. I have included some of the texts I have found most useful; and repertoire that I have encountered in my search to find pieces which satisfy both the tastes of my students, and my desires as a teacher for the student to have technical control. I've attempted to provide pieces that are satisfying musically, not overly complicated technically, and much of which can work as recital material (most of these are pieces that can work as individual pieces, or as part of a set). These may serve as alternatives to the wonderful warhorses of our repertoire, such as the Sor Etudes, Brouwer Simple Etudes, Ponce Preludes, Villa-Lobos Preludes, etc.

Most of these pieces are readily available for ordering through a sheet music retailer. The few that are a bit more difficult to find, I'd recommend trying your music library, or interlibrary loan – some of these may be out of print.

All titles are listed alphabetically by composer/author.

MEDIUM LEVEL DIFFICULTY REPERTOIRE

Oscar Ahnfelt: *Blott en dag*. This is a very successful arrangement of a 19th century hymn, with a beautiful melody and absolutely gorgeous harmonies. Relatively short, and very, very sweet. A great place to work on developing a sense of singing, and legato.

Heinrich Albert: *Sonata No. 1*. This is a neo-classical sonata in 3 movements, a nice alternative to Giuliani Opus 15 (shorter and easier than the Giuliani, in fact).

Alexander Bellow: *Suite Miniature*. This is a 5 movement, neo-Baroque suite. The prelude is a simple tremolo study; the following traditional dance suite movements are all in Baroque form but with 20th century harmonies. The level of this entire suite is very manageable, a nice work for someone who's not quite ready to tackle a suite by Bach or Weiss.

Robert Benedict: *Fughettas for Classical Guitar*. These are very enjoyable contemporary takes on a baroque form. The writing is accessible, the level is moderate. The pieces are all relatively short, and a group of a few of these pieces would make a nice set for a program, giving good practice in counterpoint without the complexity and the length involved in learning a movement (or more) of Bach.

Giuseppe Antonio Brescianello: *Sonatas and Partitas*. Brescianello wrote a series of works for a lute-like instrument called the mandora (or gallichon or calichon). These works are easier than what we typically encounter in the transcriptions of Bach, Scarlatti, etc. The mandora had the same tuning as our modern instrument (though occasionally with alternate 6th string tunings), so there is a world of relatively unknown repertoire available to us without the headache of transcription.

Frantz Casséus: *The Complete Works of Frantz Casséus: Volume 1: Music for Solo Guitar*. This is a very nice collection of pieces by the Haitian composer. These works integrate Haitian folk elements in classical music in a manner similar to that of Villa-Lobos. Most pieces in this book are fairly intermediate, and represent a type of music we don't hear much of in our standard repertoire.

Carlo Domeniconi: *Suite Caratteristica*. A suite in seven movements, using modern harmonic language, of relatively simple technical level within the intermediate range. Each movement has a distinct character, lots of nice variety, including hints at a waltz, scherzo, chorale, a couple of Latin-style movements, and a couple of very introspective movements. Very diverse musical offerings.

Roland Dyens: *Vingt Lettres*. This is a wonderful collection of 20 "letters" the composer has written, primarily in the intermediate range, some slightly easier, none of them too difficult. There is a fantastic introduction to the score, which talks about some of the finer points of playing which are often neglected – correct tuning, string damping (a favorite subject of mine), and elimination of string squeaks. The book also includes a CD. Wide range of styles, from funky to lyrical to sublime.

Mario Gangi: Various pieces. There is a nice collection of pieces (my favorites were Guitar Choro, Ametista, and Panoramica, all of which have a South American flavor) that is published by Ricordi. The Choro is reminiscent of some of Villa-Lobos' writing, but this is a bit simpler to play. Ametista is a beautiful, slow waltz; and Panoramica is a spirited piece continuing the South American feel. These three pieces (each two pages long and very manageable) work well alone or as a set. One other charming piece by Gangi, published separately, is called Con Tanta Tenerezza. This is a one page, relatively simple ballad – absolutely gorgeous, lyrical style.

Gerald Garcia: *Etudes Esquisses*. I love this collection for many reasons. They are very reasonable to handle from a technical perspective; they offer a variety of musical tastes, as well as a variety of technical tasks to master. Some are very reminiscent of the type of writing that we see in the Brouwer Simple Etudes (both in terms of harmonic language and level of difficulty), and provide a nice alternative to very common repertoire. Most of these etudes are a bit longer and more complex than the Brouwer etudes, allowing the player to feel a bit more satisfied with having learned a complete piece by learning just one etude. The last few of the set of 25 are more of a Latin feel (also a bit longer, and slightly higher level difficulty), and are a great alternative for any one loves the music of Piazzolla, but isn't quite ready to tackle that technical challenge.

Fred Hand: *Five Studies*. Beautiful American style, jazz influenced harmonies, intermediate level of difficulty. If you know and love his tune "Missing Her" (recorded by Bill Kanengiser), you'll definitely want to check into these, I think I hear the beginning ideas for that song in the third study.

Simone Iannarelli: *Cinq etudes faciles, ou presque…* This set of five etudes is very interesting. The outer movements have alternate tuning, resulting in some less than common (and very beautiful) harmonies. The first movement is a bit difficult to read due to lots of flats, but not very difficult to play – it's a good exercise in improving reading skills! Very nice musical variety between the movements, which can work alone or as a set.

Bryan Johanson: *Spring, Op. 1*; and *Simple Suite, Op. 13*. Spring is a three movement work, everything lays very comfortably under the fingers, and as its title suggests, it is a very cheerful work, I might say parts of it remind me of the general spirit of York's Sunburst. Simple Suite consists of five short movements, with a bit more chromatic edge to some of the harmonies. This is another nice alternative to the Brouwer Simple Etudes, somewhat comparable in length, difficulty and harmonic language. Simple Suite is published, Spring is not. The score for Spring can be obtained directly from the composer at: johansonb@pdx.edu.

Francis Kleynjans: *Feuillets d'Album – 10 pieces, Op. 95*. Another great collection of lesser-known pieces. These are at the upper end of the intermediate level, the reading may be a bit intimidating at first to those who aren't good sight-readers, but it is worth the work. These pieces vary in character between romantic, playful and somber; but all have gorgeous, lush harmonies that resonate beautifully on the instrument. None need to go too fast, but the left hand will be fairly busy reaching all the notes required. Also, lots of good opportunities to work on separating melody from accompaniment, and developing wonderful phrasing skills.

Luigi Legnani: *36 Caprices*, with varying levels of difficulty (some of which indeed are very virtuosic). I would recommend Nos. 1, 3, 4, 6, 12, and 28. As with any pieces, moderation in tempo is the key!

Maximo Diego Pujol: *Suites del Plata*. These two suites are both on the upper end of intermediate, with nice melodies, and good opportunities to work on steady rhythms and pulse. The first suite has an overall Latin sound to it, as does the second, with one movement diverging to a bit of blues.

Reginald Smith Brindle: *Etruscan Preludes*. This set of 5 short preludes is very lyrical in style, contemporary but accessible harmonically. The first has a distinctly Spanish character, which returns in a more veiled manner in the last prelude, which closes out the set with a hint of Rodrigo and a good strong ending, somewhat flashy. The middle three preludes have less of the Spanish sound, and are a bit more chromatic, though keeping beautiful lyricism throughout.

Milan Tesar: Four Ballad Stories. These very accessible, friendly and memorable tunes are all relatively short, and not too demanding, but produce a very nice result, reminding me in parts of some of the favorite works of Andrew York.

Traditional, arr. Scott Tennant: *Wild Mountain Thyme*. Another beautiful ballad, relatively simple, beautiful melody and harmonies.

Benjamin Verdery: *Some Towns and Cities*. This is a great collection of very catchy tunes, most of which are a bit harder than I would recommend for really working on technical and musical issues. However, there is one in here that appropriate for our purposes, and is so wonderful I couldn't leave this collection off the list. Keanae, HI is a beautiful, peaceful tune that really evokes Hawaii, and isn't that difficult to play. It has beautiful lyrical melodies, and uses a slide (yes, in a classical guitar piece!) to create that Hawaiian vibe in the middle section. Very cool piece, and very manageable. CD accompanies the book.

Andrew York: *Dreamscapes; Three Dimensions for Solo Guitar*. The Dreamscapes are a bit easier, Dimensions a bit more involved technically. Both are nice representations of the style we expect from Andrew York, and very pleasing to students and audiences alike.

Jaime Zenamon: *Preludios Poéticos*. This set of six preludes is a beautiful addition to the repertoire. The complete set would make nice programming on a recital, and individual movements also stand well on their own. Harmonic language is sort of a modern Latin American idea. Very accessible, beautiful music, with varying characters between movements.

TECHNIQUE BOOKS

Abel Carlevaro: *Serie didactica para guitarra*. A very comprehensive, in depth look at specific right and left hand issues.

Ricardo Iznaola: *Kitharologus: The Path to Virtuosity*. Not for the faint of heart, full of very challenging exercises.

Aaron Shearer: *Classic Guitar Technique, Supplement 3: Scale Pattern Studies for Guitar*. This book could be listed under technique or under sight reading, as it really is essential for both. This is a comprehensive look at scales on the guitar, including multiple exercises in many positions on the instrument, shifting scales, moveable patterns, etc. Thorough study of the materials in this book leads to a comprehensive knowledge of the fretboard, which is at the heart of good sight reading skills. When using this book for technical practice, take care not to simply practice the scales for speed- include phrasing, tone production, attention to duration of notes, and all other good listening habits when doing this or any other technical exercise.

Scott Tennant: *Pumping Nylon*. Great for speed development, and a great survey of many basic technical issues. This book is indispensable for every serious classical guitarist, a must-have.

MUSIC FOR SIGHTREADING

Béla Bartók: *44 Duos for Two Violins*. This is wonderful and enjoyable repertoire for more advanced readers. As it is not a method, nor was it written for the guitar, I would not recommend that you start here- but rather, after you've developed your approach to reading through use of one of the following methods, and you're looking to get further practice reading, this is a fun place to turn for new repertoire with a friend.

Robert Benedict: *Sightreading for the Classical Guitar*. This is a great methodical approach to sight reading. The first book may appear to be way too simple; but I highly recommend starting at the beginning, as part of what is so wonderful are all the little comments the author makes between the exercises, guiding your focus and attention towards different details of reading. The simplicity of the exercises allows you to feel confident and to read accurately. Make progress slowly and steadily for guaranteed improvement in your reading skills. Excellent book for those who have little confidence with their reading skills.

Stephen Dodgson/Hector Quine: *Progressive Reading for Guitarists*. If you think you're a good reader but want to improve, this is a good book to try. Even good readers will quickly be challenged in this comprehensive sight reading method aimed at accomplished players. The exercises explore all positions, and are a mixture of single line and multi-voice exercises, with pitches and rhythms that are not easily "predictable", and a noticeable lack of fingerings – you really have to develop your reading skills to successfully execute these exercises. This is a great book, but if you find that you aren't able to keep up with it, do your homework first by going through the Benedict books thoroughly as preparation for this.

Carlo Domeniconi: *24 Klangbilder*. These are very short and simple pieces in one and two voices, with a modern but tonal harmonic structure. They remain primarily in the first few positions, with relatively simple rhythms and a few accidentals. Excellent early material for sightreading.

Oliver Hunt: *Musicianship and Sight Reading for Guitarists*. Another wonderful methodical approach to sight reading, though this book is aimed at a more accomplished player/reader than the Benedict. Though the Hunt also begins relatively simply, the level of difficulty increases exponentially with every page (expansion in range, key and time signatures, texture, and note vote values), enough to challenge even the most accomplished reader. This book is highly recommended for all guitarists aiming at a career as performers/teachers.

Aaron Shearer: *Classic Guitar Technique, Supplement 3: Scale Pattern Studies for Guitar*. See listing under technique books.

Various: *Royal Conservatory of Music: Guitar Series*. This is a wonderful collection of pieces by various composers from various time periods. The series is divided into several levels of difficulty, for sight-reading, I'd recommend starting with the Introductory book, if that is easy, then try Level 1 or 2. This is a fun way to read through lots of repertoire while working on your reading skills.

BOOKS ON VARIOUS MUSICAL SUBJECTS

Interpretation and Performance:

Eric Booth: *The Everyday Work of Art: Awakening the Extraordinary in Your Daily Life*. This book has many nice thoughts, and primarily addresses those whose daily work is not in the arts. It encourages readers to appreciate beauty and art in daily life. It contains valuable lessons for professionals, hobbyists, and people who are not musicians/artists at all; anyone who wants to be more awake to experiences in life can get something out of this book.

Madeline Bruser: *The Art of Practicing: A Guide to Making Music from the Heart*. This is probably my favorite book on the subject of playing an instrument. The author is a pianist, but the message in universal. The book deals with some physical practicalities of playing any instrument, and primarily deals with the attitudes behind performance, and how we can develop a healthy attitude in order to reach our potential in performance. A very easy and productive read.

Edward T. Cone: *Musical Form and Musical Performance*. This is a collection of lectures that Cone made at Oberlin College in 1967. Though the book is a bit dated, the material is timeless. I find the first essay on music and its relationship to the time and space around it to be particularly interesting and accessible to most musicians. The following essays are equally wonderful, but become a bit more difficult to follow, requiring a bit more training to understand what Cone is talking about; but if you can decipher his intent, there is wonderful information there as well. The first essay alone is worth the cost of the book.

Barry Green, with Timothy Gallwey: *The Inner Game of Music*. This was the first book of its kind that I read, and there is a lot of good information here. The book asks you to do exercises, which you really need to stop and do – don't just read about them. A great book, based on the success of Gallwey's work with athletes. The goal of this book is to stop musicians from getting in their own way as they perform.

Timothy Gallwey: *The Inner Game of Tennis*. This is a wonderful book, with an even "friendlier" tone than the version adapted for musicians. The concepts are readily adaptable (you don't need to understand tennis to understand how the principles apply to you as a musician). I highly recommend this book.

Eloise Ristad: *A Soprano on Her Head: Right-side-up reflections on life and other performances*. A funny title, but another useful book on the subject of discovering your performing potential.

William Westney: *The Perfect Wrong Note: Learning to Trust Your Musical Self*. This is the most recent of all of these books (published in 2003), and is a very good addition to this category. Westney thoroughly covers healthy mental and physical approaches to both practice and performance.

Historical Performance Practice:

Clive Brown: *Classical and Romantic Performing Practice 1750-1900*. The same idea as the Donington books, but covering a different period of music. This book covers similar topics, but instead giving us the ideas that were common to composers from Mozart to Brahms and beyond. This book is significantly longer than the Donington, in part because it covers more territory, but also in part because he incorporates a bit more historical perspective. You'll have to dig more to get to the information that will help you as a performer, but it is all there.

Thurston Dart: *The Interpretation of Music*. This is a very manageable book in terms of length (less than 200 pages), and very easy to read. Dart provides a couple of chapters that are wonderful food for thought regarding putting historical performance in perspective. Topics covered in the book include tone color, pitch, and acoustical surroundings at the time of composition; our current attitude of strictly abiding by the score versus the practice of extemporization; and style in 18th century, 17th century, Renaissance and Middle Ages (no discussion of 19th century).

Robert Donington: *A Performer's Guide to Baroque Music*. The title of this book says it all. Written by a musicologist, but with performers in mind. This book addresses many practical issues that come up for performers in the study of Baroque music, including feeling, style, sound, accidentals, ornamentation, tempo, rhythm, and dynamics.

Robert Donington: *The Interpretation of Early Music*. This is similar in content to A Performer's Guide to Baroque Music, but this book is significantly longer. If you want every last detail of Donington's impressive knowledge on this subject, this is the book for you. Donington extensively includes citations from primary sources (CPE Bach, Quantz, Couperin, etc.), making this a very valuable resource.

Music Theory and the Guitar:

Robert Lilienfeld and Basil Cimino: *The Guitarist's Theory Guide: An Elementary Textbook on Harmony for* *the Guitar.* A workbook type format covering same basic materials as the Shearer. This book gets a bit complicated, intended more for the person who is very seriously interested in the subject. One big plus to this book, it has an appendix at the back with exercises for each chapter that are playing examples, fingered on the guitar, illustrating the concépts covered. Truly, these are solutions to exercises in the chapters; but they serve as a great way to work out your understanding of the concepts.

Aaron Shearer: *Classic Guitar Technique, Supplement 2: Basic Elements of Music Theory for the Guitar.* Workbook type format, guides you through basic elements of theory (whole and half steps, scales, intervals, and chords). A great basic introduction to theory, though not necessarily with any strong ties to the instrument.

ABOUT THE AUTHOR

The *Illinois Times* wrote that guitarist Martha Masters "…is on a swift and certain trajectory to star territory." Masters' playing has been described as "seductive" (*Ft. Worth Star Telegram*), "intelligent and natural" (*Guitar Review*), and "refined and elegant" (*American Record Guide*). She has received critical acclaim as a solo recitalist, as a chamber musician with Duo Erato, and as a soloist with orchestras. Recent concert seasons have included performances on concert series and at festivals in England, Denmark, Spain, Poland, Germany, Paraguay, Peru, Puerto Rico, Canada, Mexico, and numerous US cities. Martha's first CD, *Serenade*, is now in its second printing, and her Naxos recital disc sold over 10,000 copies worldwide in the first year of its release. She has three recordings on the GSP label, and a disc with duo partner Risa Carlson.

In October of 2000 Martha won first prize in the Guitar Foundation of America (GFA) International Solo Competition, including a recording contract with Naxos, a concert video with Mel Bay, and an extensive North American concert tour. In November of 2000, she also won the Andrés Segovia International Guitar Competition in Linares, Spain and was a finalist in the Alexandre Tansman International Competition of Musical Personalities in Lodz, Poland. Prior to 2000, Martha was a prizewinner or finalist in numerous other international competitions, including the 1999 International Guitar Competition "Paco Santiago Marín" in Granada, Spain, the 1998 Tokyo International Guitar Competition and the 1997 GFA International Solo Competition.

In addition to leading the guitar program at Loyola Marymount University in Los Angeles and extensive masterclass/festival teaching, Martha teaches annually at the National Guitar Workshop Classical Summit in Connecticut, and on WorkshopLive.com. She is also Executive Director of the Guitar Foundation of America (GFA), dedicated to supporting the instrument, its players and its music in the US and throughout the world.

Martha received both the Bachelor and Master of Music degrees from the Peabody Conservatory, where she studied with Manuel Barrueco, and completed the Doctor of Musical Arts degree at the University of Southern California as a student of Scott Tennant.